the UNDERGROUND GUIDE to SPARTANBURG

- VOL. 2 -

EDITED BY JOE MULLINAX

*This book is
dedicated to
the folks who
keep it fresh.
You know
who you are.*

First printing, August 2015

Cover design: Russell Bannan, Meg Reid & Aimee Wise

Interior design: Brandy Lindsey & The Graphics House

Assistant editor: Betsy Teter

Proofreader: Mary Therese Jackson

Printed in the United States of America

The Underground Guide to Spartanburg Vol. 2 is
funded by grants from the City of Spartanburg and the
Spartanburg Convention and Visitors Bureau.

ISBN: 978-1-938235-14-6

186 West Main Street
Spartanburg, SC 29306
www.hubcity.org

contents

welcome TO VOLUME 2!

The first time we did this book it was immensely popular. So much so that we sold out. We then took all that info and put it on a website so you could keep discovering Spartanburg's Underground. Three years after the first publication, much has changed in Spartanburg. As a result we've added close to 60 new entrees in this edition: from craft beer to acupuncture, from the dog park to fishin' holes, from smoothie stores to apple farms. We've updated dozens of others.

We're here to tell you there's a lot more to Spartanburg than you might otherwise have heard. Sure, there's a lot of old cotton mills and and railroads and Revolutionary War battle sites around. And the Carolina Panthers come to town in the summer, and we just might have more onion rings per capita than anywhere else. But there's a lot more. The things we like to do often don't show up in the official tourist publications. We don't want you to miss the soulful and funky sides of our city—our favorite hangouts and hikes, the places we go for vintage clothing, disc golf, and guitar strings. We want you to know where you can get a meal after midnight, where the loudest music is, and where the scene is jumping.

Did we include everything? No. Have we missed some things? Certainly, but this is a good list to get you started. You'll notice that some prominent things in town are not included, like the Chapman Cultural Center,

Westgate Mall and the pricey restaurants, just to name a few. Well, those places aren't really underground. It's not the purpose of this book to point out the obvious. Pick up a copy of the Visitors Guide from the Spartanburg Convention & Visitors Bureau for that. There is some great stuff in there. Stuff that your mom will like, and perhaps you too, but this is a different kind of guidebook. We chose to focus on things out of the ordinary with an emphasis on free— or at least cheap—fun.

I grew up here and thought I knew this place inside and out, but I learned about lots of places I wasn't aware of while working on this project. Cool places, odd places, places I'm going to take my friends to visit. I wish I'd had a copy of this book when we were in high school, or home from college, when the mantra was always "there's nothing to do in Spartanburg." Things have certainly changed. I hope what you're holding in your hands becomes a well-worn copy so that you never have to utter that phrase.

Everything in this guide is in Spartanburg unless otherwise noted. The street addresses and zip codes are there for you to drop into your GPS.

We haven't designed itineraries or put together lists of things for you to do. Instead we've organized the book by topics. When you are ready to chow, crack open the book and try a new spot. When you are looking to get outdoors, crack open the book and find adventure. When it's time to find where the locals hang, crack it open and come have a drink with us.

Keep crackin'.
We'll see you out there,

Joe C. Mullinax
Editor

From fine wine to local brews, we give you the lowdown on wetting your whistle. Get out there and be social.

WILD WINGS | *109 W. Main St, 29306*

Look, everyone wants the same things in life: atomic hot wings, two-dollar drafts on Tuesdays, bingo night on Wednesdays, $2.50 house liquor with a DJ spinning beats on Thursdays, Friday nights full of live, rocking music, Saturdays with more live music happening all around you. That's why we have a place like Wild Wings. The balcony overlooking Morgan Square is the choice imbibing spot in the spring and fall. (864) 585-4646, Mon-Sun 11am-2am.

REFUEL WINE BAR AND RETAIL | *129 N. Spring St, 29302*

Located in one of downtown's restored historic buildings, Refuel Wine Bar and Retail offers a chic environment where you'll find more than 30 labels available for purchase and 13 wines available by the glass. A full bar offers a variety of mixed drinks, including their specialty, the Perfect Manhattan. Sumptuous tapas meals are served on biodegradable dinnerware. There's live music on weekends. (864) 529-7892. Tues-Sat, 5-9pm. *refuelwinebarandretail.com*

Like dive bars? Don't miss the Nu-Way, the oldest and best bar in town.

NU-WAY | *373 E. Kennedy St, 29302*

There are dive bars, and then there's the Nu-Way. Spartanburg's oldest bar, the Nu-Way has been in continuous operation since 1938, quenching the thirsts and satiating the appetites of generations of Spartanburg residents. Delightfully unpretentious and fashionably unfashionable, the bar is everything a great bar should be, from the sagging ceiling tiles to the Christmas lights and neon signs that provide most of the venue's lighting at night.

During the day, the Nu-Way serves up lunch, including its award-winning Redneck Cheeseburger (topped with lettuce, tomato, onion, chili, mustard, mayonnaise, and pimento cheese), called the best burger in South Carolina by *Food Network* magazine. At night though, the Nu-Way caters to a different, younger crowd looking more for a cold beer than a hot burger.

Owner Becky Hammond-Myers, who bought the Nu-Way in 2005 after working the bar for six years, says what sets the Nu-Way apart is its special place in the lives of so many of Spartanburg's residents. "I think that everybody has a Nu-Way story, just some people don't want to admit it," she reveals. In addition to serving up drinks, the Nu-Way also serves as one of Spartanburg's best music venues with local and regional favorites setting up in a corner of the bar (there is no stage), playing sets for the truly enthusiastic music-loving crowds for which the Nu-Way is known. (864) 582-9685, Mon-Fri 11am-2am, Sat 11am-midnight.

THE BOILING SPRINGS ALE HOUSE | *2220 Boiling Springs Rd, 29316*

Sometimes you get surprised. Though you consider yourself a beer aficionado, you find four beers out of twenty on the draft menu you've never heard of. You order the calamari expecting it to be out of a frozen bag like most places, but instead it's fresh with a light delicate breading and so delicious. You glance at the menu and see the usual offerings of sliders, wings and burgers, then see a variety of shish kabobs. Your order took a while to come out, so the chef brings you fried pickles and handcut fries on the house to hold you over. Whoa.

The Ale House seems to have surprised Boiling Springs as well when it opened in 2014, and folks are loving it. And why not? A piano player mid-week for ladies night, and bands on Thursday, Friday and Saturdays with sounds ranging from jazz to country to classic rock. They roll out a stage with a light rig for the bands. And they do big events in the parking lot like bike rallies and poker runs that really pack the place. Plus it's your game-day headquarters with an 80-inch TV over the bar and 14 others throughout the place, including the bathrooms. The craft beer selection rotates and there are plenty of options in this well-stocked bar.

So go see Amy, the bartender, order a drink you've never tried and try not to act too surprised at how much fun you're having in Boiling Springs. (864) 308-8898, Mon/Tues 3pm-midnight, Wed-Sat 11:30-2am, Sun 11:30am-midnight. *boilingsprings-alehouse.com*

Don't be surprised if there are lots of brews you've never heard of. Belly up to the bar and let the adventure begin.

GROWLER HAUS \ *113 N. Church St, 29306*

Craft beer is as omnipresent as kudzu these days, but up until recently, Spartanburg had no place committed to its consumption. Then 2012 brought us the Growler Haus. Sure, the game may be on, but the real draw is behind the bar. Growler Haus has two dozen taps of the finest craft beer with an emphasis on U.S. breweries. Tour the time zones with a Californian Indian Pale Ale, a stout from the Rocky Mountains, a Michigan lager, and end with one of our local South Carolina brews like Charleston's Holy City or our own RJ Rockers. The beer menu changes frequently, so pop in to take a look at the chalkboard or check out the current line-up on their website, complete with ratings and reviews from sites like Beer Advocate and Rate Beer.

Additionally, Growler Haus offers a wide selection of canned and bottled beer, including bombers. Of course, growlers are always available to fill up and take home. Seating is ample with armchairs, couches and an expansive outdoor patio. The bartenders are happy to offer sip-sized samples, and if you're not quite up for a full glass of Southern Tier's Creme Brulee Stout or Green Flash's aptly-named Palette Wrecker, ask for a half-pour. This a bar for beer people, by beer people, so ask questions, get recommendations and don't be shy—just don't order a Bud Lite, and you'll be fine. (864) 585-6000, Mon 4:30-11pm, Tues & Wed 3-10pm, Thurs 3-11pm, Fri & Sat noon-11pm. *growlerhaus.com*

THE MUSIC STAND AT BLUES BOULEVARD

99 S. Church St, 29306

This place has hosted some of the best blues and jazz acts in a multi-state area. New owner, Patrick Moss, is continuing this tradition. He is a trumpet player who has performed with members of the James Brown Band. He's a Spartanburg native who has returned home after a long career in the military and wants the live music scene to be jumpin'. Look for jazz jam sessions on the weekends and acts throughout the week. Wed-Thur 5pm-11pm, Fri-Sat 5-until.

MAIN STREET PUB | *252 W. Main St, 29306*

Main Street Pub is a great place to go for good food and drinks without drying out your wallet. The crowd there varies, but at night, it's a younger pack, with a mix of young professionals and Spartanburg's art crowd. If you're into karaoke, then you'll want to be there Tuesday nights. Bring your A-game, as you'll find singers who also are also active in local theatre. Or just come and listen. They'll have live music some nights, DJ music some nights and sports on the TVs especially Sunday and Monday (though this pub does not have the feel of a sports bar). (864) 573-1165, Mon 4pm-midnight, Tues-Fri 4pm-2am, Sat 3pm-2am, Sun 3pm-midnight.

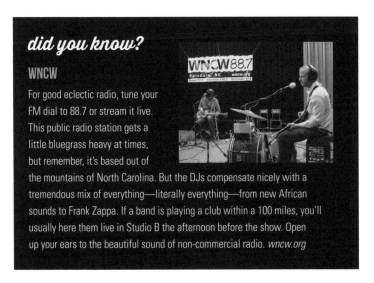

did you know?

WNCW

For good eclectic radio, tune your FM dial to 88.7 or stream it live. This public radio station gets a little bluegrass heavy at times, but remember, it's based out of the mountains of North Carolina. But the DJs compensate nicely with a tremendous mix of everything—literally everything—from new African sounds to Frank Zappa. If a band is playing a club within a 100 miles, you'll usually here them live in Studio B the afternoon before the show. Open up your ears to the beautiful sound of non-commercial radio. *wncw.org*

GROUNDZERO | *3052 Howard St, 29303*

For ear-shattering punk, metal, indie and even hip-hop, GroundZero is the setting for Spartanburg's most intense nightlife. Here, you can often see the heaviest bands in the world—some that otherwise appear in stadiums—with two or three hundred enthusiastic fans. Kid Rock has played here. So has Slayer and David Allen Coe. Loud and fast, the club is a mecca for music fans sick of Northface jackets and cover songs so common in other local venues. Cover is cheap and the alcohol is, too, though cash only.

The club is nestled on one of Howard Street's bleaker stretches. Inside you'll find an open room dominated by a stage with a bar off to the side. The air is thick with cigarette smoke and young hope. When the music cranks up, be ready for a maelstrom of flailing limbs in front of GZ's no-frills stage. Burley Mick Minchow has run this place since 1996, motivated by his desire to help out emerging local musicians. "We wanted a place for our friends' bands to play," he says rather humbly.

Truth is, he is a tireless advocate for cutting-edge original music.

This isn't some over-priced spot for wine-swilling suits and pencil skirts to come talk market strategies. This is Spartanburg's true underground. (864) 948-1661, Wed-Thurs 6pm-2am, Fri 6pm-5am, Sat 6pm-midnight.

When you are ready to rock, Ground Zero is ready for you. Gas mask optional.

No shortage of choices at this Irish bar that's great for late-night imbibing.

DELANEY'S IRISH PUB | *117 W. Main St, 29306*

We could say any number of different things about this pub. We could mention that it's on Morgan Square, that it hosts live music regularly with no cover charge, trivia (bar tab partly covered for the winner) and Wednesday night Pint Nights featuring $2 beers. (If it's on tap, it's $2, and yes, that includes Guinness. Starts at 9 and ends when you do.)

On the menu at Delaney's is everything from fried mushrooms to Shepherd's Pie to even a decent filet. (BOGO meals on Mondays, brunch on Sunday.) But it wouldn't be an Irish Pub if there weren't darts. You find those on the way to the Green Mile (a stretch of hallway leading you to the bathrooms). If that's not your thing, there are 15 HD televisions playing all kinds of sports. But what you really need to know about this place, beyond all the college students who frequent it and make you feel like your 20s are only a Jager-bomb away, is that they have more than 30 beers on tap. Thirty beers. On tap. So, grab your handbags and put on your drinking shoes, because Wednesday happens every week, and all you need is a ten-spot to start the night off right. (864) 583-3100, Mon-Fri 11am-2am, Sat 11am-midnight. *delaneyspubsc.com*

*Boys just wanna have fun, and
sometimes that means being in a drag show.*

CLUB SOUTH 29 | *9112 Greenville Hwy, 29301*

Are you looking for a LGBT-friendly environment to let your hair down
and have good time? Are you looking to dance the night away in a setting
complete with a live DJ, great sounding digital audio system, full lighting
array and large projection screen providing a live view of the action
for everyone in the club to see? Then Club South 29 is your place.

In addition to the large dance area, Club South 29 also features an
upstairs "Skybox" lounge (with its own bar) that's more laid back, but
still offers a view of the action downstairs. On the live entertainment
front, Club South 29 features live musical acts, drag shows and theme
nights as varied as the colors of the rainbow. Saturday is definitely the
night to check out Club 29. The later the hour, the more the club heats
up with the scantily clad "South 29 Boys" taking the stage and dancing
on the bar. Owner Andy Tinsley sums up the Club South 29 experience
well, saying, "We try to have a party atmosphere every weekend." You
can be sure, there's no place in Spartanburg with a party atmosphere
quite like this. This is a membership club and you can sign up at the
door, but fill it out ahead of time online so you can drink alcohol that
evening. (864) 574-6087, Fri-Sat, 9pm-3am. *clubsouth29.com*

HUB CITY TAP HOUSE: HOME OF CICLOPS CYDERI

197 E. St. John St, 29302

Spartanburg's newest brewery is also a winery and a cidery, and the good folks here have adopted the slogan "Making Absurd the Norm." That's because an ex-chef is in charge of the unique concoctions moving through its three-barrel brewing system: beverages with lychee fruit, kaffir limes, coffee and the like. There's a 40-foot bar, 30 taps with regional brews, and beer for sale in growlers and bombers. You'll find a cool indoor mural, cold-style appetizers and a European pub atmosphere. Stop by and meet the enthusiastic proprietors, Michael Willcox and Kolby Garrison. (864) 704-9080, Tues-Thurs 3-10pm, Fri & Sat noon-midnight.

THE PEDDLER | *Town Square, 464 E. Main St, 29302*

Yes, it's a steakhouse, but it's also one of the best spots to hear live music in town, though only on Wednesdays. The bar is busy on the weekends, and on Wednesday nights you can often hear legendary troubadour David Ezell, who's been called "Spartanburg's Pete Seeger." Homegrown musicians love this place because of its acoustics and cozy atmosphere. There's an old cigarette machine in the corner, stripped boxing trunks on the wall and a dented tuba suspended above the bar. If you're hungry, well, there's steaks. Good ones. (864) 583-5874, Mon-Thurs 4-9:30pm; Fri-Sat 4-10pm. *peddlerspartanburg.com*

did you know?

THE HOP SPOT   *194 E. Henry St, 29302*

You know you'll find beer in a convenience store, but this may be the only c-store that has two lowly shelves for Budweiser and fills the rest of the Beer Cave with over 220 craft beers. This is literally the best, ice-cold selection of brews in town. Local and regional selections are clearly marked and promoted. Because the selection can be a bit daunting, they've provided write ups on the beers including descriptions, origin, ABV and ratings. No wonder they changed one of the signs out front from Hot Spot to Hop Spot. (864) 583-5508, open 24 hours.

We love a bar with no windows. 2pm and 2am look the same.

THE UPSTAIRS BAR | *198 Ezell St, 29306*

Still thirsty at 3 a.m.? The Upstairs Bar is the place you are looking for in downtown Spartanburg. This local watering hole now boasts a golfing arcade game, laser light show Mondays, a mural of the old Spartanburg skyline and a super special specialty drink: Chelsea's Blueberry Goodness Shot. Craving cocktails and local music? Look no further. The Upstairs Bar features musical guests every weekend. Some of the special house drinks include the Irish Coffee Martini, the Mocha, the Ginger Weed, the Maple and the Coupe De Ville. What more could you want? A two-dollar PBR? You got it.

If you catch a case of the munchies, the Upstairs Bar is conveniently attached to the Brickhouse Pizzeria and you have full access to their menu until 10pm. Come on Monday or Tuesday and you might catch Comedy Night happening in the pizzeria downstairs. (864) 585-0555, Mon-Fri 4pm-4am, Sat/Sun 4pm-2am.

SHOW US YOUR TALENT!

Sunday at Brickhouse Pizzeria & Grille (103 Daniel Morgan Ave.) is singer/songwriter night founded and hosted by resident musician, Jamison Smith. There is an open mic from 7:30 to 8:30, then a featured artist plays for an hour or so, followed by more open mic. The night caters to original music, but doesn't discriminate against covers during open mic. It generally focuses on songwriters of all genres, but bands make appearances as well. It's a diverse night of music that can showcase musicians of all ages playing everything from folk to rock to soul to pop. So get out and show the world what you've got!

GERHARD'S CAFÉ \ *1200 E. Main St, 29307*

The sign outside proclaims Gerhard's Café to be a banquet room, a restaurant, a bar and a pizzeria all in one, and while that kind of approach is usually a recipe for disaster, Gerhard's makes it work. On any given night there's likely a who's who of Spartanburg business leaders eating wiener schnitzel and sipping martinis in the restaurant, while a contingent of college students eats brick-oven pizza and drinks Warsteiner. With a style and atmosphere to suit almost anyone, Gerhard's is an eclectic gem on Spartanburg's east side. (864) 591-1920, Mon-Sat 5:30pm-10pm. *gerhardscafe.net*

DUDLEY'S \

1055B Fernwood Glendale Rd, 29307

Come for the massive patio and stay for the American Cuisine. If you sit inside, the grille is right at the bar and you get to watch as your steak, chicken or fish is prepared. Try the rib eye sandwich or the low-country boil and once you're done with those, check out the Martini Bar. (864) 573-2626, Mon-Fri 4pm-midnight, Sat/Sun 1pm-midnight. *dudleysonline.com*

HICKORY TAVERN \

143 Fernwood Dr, 29307

With a low-lit atmosphere, this place is as much restaurant as it is a bar and music venue. Performers cover everything from '80s rock to acoustic singer/songwriter acts. Patrons range from college to middle-aged and the bar offers over 60 beers and a variety of wines. The full menu ranges from tacos to shrimp-and-grits, making it a good choice for anyone who's getting hungry for more than fast food after a couple of drinks. (864) 591-3290, Mon-Fri 4pm-2am, Sat 11:30am-2am, Sun 11:30am-midnight. *thehickorytavern.com*

did you know?

DRINKING LIBERALLY

There's no doubt about it: it's tough to be a liberal in the buckle of the Bible Belt. So what's the alienated politico with a penchant for tasty beverages to do when looking for camaraderie? Join the folks at Drinking Liberally's Spartanburg branch for their get-togethers every Tuesday night about 6pm. Started in June 2008, the group currently takes up residence at the Nu-Way Lounge, 373 East Kennedy Street. "We are not activists ... We are the social arm of the progressive movement," says group co-founder Cass Chulick. *livingliberally.org/drinking/chapters/SC/spartanburg*

Support local ... drink the brew that is made here.

RJ ROCKERS BREWERY | *226 W. Main St, 29306*

Hands down, this is the place to be on Thursday, Friday and Saturday afternoons. Sometimes it seems like the whole town has come to Tour & Taste, where your first pint is $5 and includes an RJ Rockers pint glass, and refills are $4. There's music on the loading dock on Fridays (Hoppy Hour), and you can get the full tour of this microbrewery famous for its Son of a Peach signature beer.

Depending on the time of the year, here's some of what's on tap: Witty Twister, First Snow, Brown Eyed Squirrel, Bell Ringer (8% ABV), Gruntled Pumpkin, Strawberry Bomber and Black Perle (9.5%!). The Good Boy Stout is named after the Rockers mascot, a jowly black lab who's every bit at home here as the hard-working brew crew.

Formerly the home of the Salvation Army, this solar-powered microbrewery has a 30-barrel brewing system with a capacity for 25,000 barrels. Gulf War veteran Mark Johnsen started Rockers as a tiny Morgan Square brew pub in 1997, and it continues to grow every year. Son of a Peach has been spotted in specialty beer stores all over the United States. You can also find their beers fresh and on tap in bars throughout Spartanburg. But the best way to experience this brewery is with the crowd that gathers in the afternoons, so drop what you're doing and head down to the place "where beer is an art." (864) 585-BEER, Thurs-Fri 3-7:30pm, Sat noon-4pm. *rjrockers.com*

CARRIAGE HOUSE WINES | *196 W. Main St, 29306*

Located in the heart of downtown Spartanburg is a wine store in a charming brick building that housed a wagon factory way back in 1900. This isn't a wine store to simply pick up a bottle and go; Carriage House is a place to meet, eat an appetizer or two (they do some light dishes) and uncork a bottle to enjoy on site. With a bar backed by exposed red brick, Carriage House is both elegant and subtle. If you're not up for wine, then try some of their handpicked, well-crafted and high gravity beers. Still, the wine here is the star. Owner Tony Forest has been in the wine business 28 years, and whether you're looking for something inexpensive or perhaps considering a more pricey bottle, he is there to help you out.

"Wine is much like music, in that it is subjective," Tony says. "You have to find a style that suits your taste. There are no wrong styles. It all depends on what you find tasty and interesting." Carriage House holds tastings, many of them free, for the public as well as for private groups. Dates for public tastings are on their website and fees for private events can be found there, too. But go early; Carriage House is a place for afternoon drinking. (864) 582-0123, Mon-Fri 11am-7pm, Sat 11am-4pm. *carriagehousewines.com*

Tony's always popping a cork, either for you to sample or to enjoy a bottle with your friends.

GREER OPRY HOUSE | *107 Cannon St, Greer 29651*

If you're hankering for some authentic country dance music and find yourself halfway between Spartanburg and Greenville, the Greer Opry House is as good a bet as you're likely to find. The building (formerly a skating rink) is brick and nondescript, but the marquee sign is straight out of Austin, Texas. Nine dollars gets you in the door on either weekend night for live music, but Saturday is the night to go if you're looking for the classic country sound, à la Waylon Jennings and George Jones. Crowds sometimes top 150 people.

Owner Peggy Stewart says tour groups and visitors often wander in. "There was a Legends Show—we had Loretta and Conway that night—and this group of people from England had a blast. It was unreal," she recalls. The place is a regular museum of country music artifacts, including pieces of banjos once owned by Lester Flatt and Earl Scruggs and signed photos of Johnny Cash, June Carter and others. "My late husband was a Dolly freak," Peggy adds.

There's a strict no-alcohol policy, but sodas are available to quench the thirst you'll work up after cutting a rug on the venue's large wooden dance floor.

(864) 801-1999, Fri-Sat 8-11pm. *greeropryhouse.5u.com*

When you want to put on your boots and do the two-step, head to the Opry House.

THE MUSIC CAMP

What if we told you a local hippie bought a bunch of land known as "Hell's Half Acre" in Cowpens beside the Pacolet River and over the course of 15+ years has built a big stage and covered seating area and hosts concerts featuring local and regional acts. And that these are weekend-long events where everyone camps, hangs at the river during the day and parties all night. Would you wanna go? Of course you would. Events are sporadic, but when they happen you don't wanna miss it. *themusiccamp.net*

MOONSHINERS REUNION

"We're sort of the outlaws of bluegrass," said Barney Barnwell, founder of two music festivals at Plum Hollow Farm. As much a cultural celebration as anything else, the Moonshiners Reunion & Mountain Music Festival (first weekend in October) celebrates the heritage of folk music and the history of moonshining near South Carolina's "Dark Corner." This 50-acre farm north of Spartanburg also hosts the Plum Hollow Alternative Bluegrass Festival the last weekend in May. Bring your instruments for the jam sessions. Big beard and overalls not required, but if you have 'em, you'll fit right in. *moonshiners.com*

JAM IN THE PARK

Pack a cooler, grab the dog, round up some friends and plan to spend the day at Duncan Pak on Union Street. Started by local bands that wanted to let their family and friends hear them play without having to be at the Nu-Way till 2 am, this concert series has been going on for a handful of years, and each year it gets bigger and better. Happens at the amphitheatre on occasional Sunday afternoons, and best of all, it's free. *jaminthepark.com*

NCG CINEMAS | *1985 E. Main St, 29307*

When you feel like watching a movie but don't want to battle the traffic of Westgate Mall (where there are two cineplexes inexplicably within a mile of one another), you have options. On the east side, located at the Hillcrest Shopping Center, is NCG Cinemas, which offers eight screens of high-def cinematic glory. There's nothing not to love about this theater: the seats are recliners, the aisles are clean and prices are budget-friendly (like $5 Tuesdays). The lobby provides a touch-screen Coke Freestyle machine with a dazzling array of choices. Mix your own soft drink cocktail—Peach Mello Yello and vanilla Dr. Pepper with a splash of Grape Hi-C, anyone? Grab that free refill and enjoy the show. (864) 764-1315. *ncgmovies.com/spartanburg*

FAMILY VIDEO | *1392 W.O. Ezell Blvd, 29301*

Across from a pawn shop and next door to a massage parlor stands a bastion of American history: the video store. In the onslaught of online options, Family Video is not only surviving, but absolutely thriving. They've recently remodeled and added an in-store Marco's Pizza. There are no membership fees or cards, no email blasts or promotional giveaways. Family Video is refreshingly old school, with a full range of new releases and an impressive— if erratic—collection of older movies. Ask about specials, as Family Video rewards those who rent in bulk. Most movies, if you fall in love, can be purchased after renting. For the gamer, Family Video offers video games for all current consoles, including handhelds. Watch out for late fees, though the price is worth it for the experience of idle movie store browsing, nearly extinct in the age of Netflix. 10am-midnight. (864) 595-2929. *familyvideo.com*

WYNNSONG SEVEN | *1640 John B White Sr Blvd, 29301*

Spartanburg's only second-run theater is Wynnsong Seven. What are the perks of a second-run theater? The full movie experience of big screens and surround sound at less than half the price. These are films that haven't quite made it to Redbox yet. Inside, there's pinball, arcade games and a claw prize machine, and the concession stands offer Stimulus Tuesday packages with affordable soda and popcorn. Matinees are $2 on weekdays and only $1.50 on Saturdays; evening shows aren't much more at $2.50. And, if you're looking for the V.I.P. treatment, you can rent an entire theater for yourself and some friends. (864) 576-3240. *carmike.com*

HUB DIGGITY \ *201-B Wall St, 29306*

Connecticut native Bobby Beauvais has expanded his once walk-up hot dog stand into some new digs (pun intended) and it's better than ever. The new location still features their classic brats served on pretzel rolls and Nathan's Famous hot dogs, along with new menu items, including salads and veggie dogs. On Fridays and Saturdays, try the New England Lobster Roll, made with a half pound of 100 percent pure lobster meat on a toasted bun. Better get there early—people come from all around to get this authentic New England treat. (864) 310-4426, Mon-Wed 11am-3pm, Thur 11am-7pm (seasonal), Fri 11am-6pm, Sat 11am-3pm.

McCLELLAN'S \ *253 Magnolia St, 29306*

If you want to go uptown with your meat-and-three, McClellan's Urban Eatery is an unexpected surprise in Spartanburg's legal district. Chef Bill McClellan is bringing "Southern cuisine with a French twist" to the city with this bright and quaint, 50-seat restaurant that opened mid-2015. You know it's good when the kitchen is bigger than the restaurant! (The chef is a favorite local caterer so he needs the room.) Artwork on the walls, of African-American life in Spartanburg, is by Spartanburg's own Raymond Floyd. (864) 707-5554, Mon-Tues 11am-4pm; Wed-Fri 8am-9pm; Sunday brunch 11am-4pm. *mcclellaneatery.com*

VENUS PIE | *400 E. Main St, 29302*

You know those pizza joints where you walk in and immediately want to order a pitcher of beer to go with that delicious pie? This is one of those joints. It looks like many a good time has been had in Venus Pie since they opened in 1995. There's an open kitchen where you can watch the guys toss the dough while you are racking up a high score on the pinball machine. There's also a combo arcade game: Ms. Pac Man AND Galaga. The owners, who can usually be found behind the register, have put their personality into the place with all the memorabilia on the walls, from old record covers to sports jerseys.

This is New York style pie and that's what you'll find on the menu. Want something else? Spinach salad is your other choice. A whole pizza too much for lunch? Order a single slice, which is huge, and pile it high with toppings. Calzones are also a favorite here, too (which is really just a folded up pizza, isn't it?).The food is great and cheap, with a slice of cheese for $2.75.

And the place has its own stupid criminals' trivia: once a burglar got stuck upside down in the hood system, trying to break in from the roof! (864) 582-4200, Tues-Thu 11:30am-2pm and 5-9pm, Fri 11:30am-2pm and 5-10pm, Sat 11:30am-10pm.

WILD ACE PIZZA AND PUB | *148 W. Main St, 29306*

Lots of cool things going on at this pizza place. First off, it's in an old Citizens & Southern Bank. Now it has World War replica planes hanging from the ceiling as part of the restaurant's aviation theme. Then there is the "green" aspect with a solar-powered water heater on the roof along with LED lighting. And most important is the delicious New York style pizza and great selection of craft beer. You can get a single slice for $1.99. With two floors, seating for 250 and a nice outdoor dining area right on Morgan Square, you're sure to find a spot. (864) 764-1480, Mon-Sat 11am-11pm, Sun noon-9pm. *thewildace.com*

APOLLO'S HOUSE OF PIZZA | *8151 Warren Abernathy Hwy, 29301*

Judging by the name, one might not expect that Apollo's House of Pizza would have classic Greek offerings like hummus and pita bread, souvlaki and spanakopita on the menu, but those offerings are the establishment's real stars. Of course, you could just split the difference and order the Greek spaghetti, a dish of spaghetti noodles tossed in extra virgin olive oil, Greek spices and feta cheese. (864) 587-7114, Mon-Thurs 11am-10pm, Fri/Sat 11am-11pm. *apolloshouseofpizza.com*

BRICKHOUSE PIZZERIA & GRILL | *103 S. Daniel Morgan Ave, 29306*

Right off downtown's Main Street strip, Brickhouse Pizza serves up a fine array of RJ Rockers beers on tap, and, of course, probably the best wood-fired pizza you're going to find within a hundred miles. On Tuesdays there's 2-for-1 pizza, and Thursdays, all-you-can-eat spaghetti for $4.99. Join the crowd for trivia on Wednesdays. There's a fantastic outdoor patio to boot. (864) 585-0555, Mon-Sat 11:30am-10pm, Sun 4:30-10pm.

MELLOW MUSHROOM | *464 E. Main St, 29302*

Technically a chain based out of Atlanta, the Mellow Mushroom location in Spartanburg feels like a local place and is embraced as such by a loyal following in town. Renowned for their "spring-water dough" pizza crust and quirky names for specialty pizzas like Magical Mystery Tour, Kosmic Karma and Philosopher's Pie, a trip to Mellow Mushroom is great pizza served in a place that strives hard to maintain an offbeat sensibility. (864) 582-5495, Mon-Thurs 11am-10pm, Fri & Sat 11am-11pm, Sun noon-9pm. *mellowmushroom.com/spartanburg*

BAGUETTE & CO. | *201 Wall St, 29306*

It's the taste of the old world, from crêpes to pastries, at this corner bakery & bistro with serious French bona fides. Veronique Bellfontaine, from France, and her husband, John, whose mother is French, make European-style goodies, including their famous baguettes (hard crust, soft inside) with a special flour blend that took them a year to refine.

Le petit café has a turret-style bay window overlooking City Hall, comfy stools, and a chess set for those who want to while away the day amid the aroma of freshly baked bread. At the pastry counter, you'll find delicious buttermilk scones, crème puffs, éclairs, honey buns and more. There's specialty coffee, and a big basket of baguettes. At lunch time, the Bellfontaines offer la Parisienne Cubano (their signature meal), various sandwiches on flaky croissants, and vegetarian couscous. The dinner menu includes a variety of crêpes—be sure to try the chicken and apple brandy! And on Saturday mornings, the full spread of breads is revealed.

The mothership bakery is located in downtown Cowpens, at 5326

S. Main St. Look for the yellow building with the blue roof at the only stoplight in Cowpens. All the baking takes place here, and it is open to the public for shopping or an afternoon meal Fridays and Saturdays, noon-4pm.

On top of all this, the Bellfontaines will even take you to France with them on their annual holiday. Ask at the counter when the next trip is leaving. (864) 216-8123, Tues/Wed 8am-3pm, Thurs-Sat 8am-3pm and 5:30-9pm.

WARNING: these cupcakes are very addictive!

CAKEHEAD BAKESHOP | 188 W. Main St, 29306

Occasionally, we, as a community, get lucky. And that's exactly what happened when Liz Blanchard, who grew up on the Gulf Coast, decided to open up her very own bakery in downtown's old Masonic temple. Located in the back of the Little River Coffee Bar, Cakehead Bakeshop provides an assortment of gourmet scones, quiches, cupcakes, pies, cookies, lemon bars, turnovers, wedding cakes—well, you get the idea. If you need something sweet, there is honestly nothing better. Not here. Not anywhere.

By all means, don't miss a visit to Cakehead during Mardi Gras. That's when the crew creates steaming hot beignets and colorful king cakes, complete with the plastic baby Jesus. And if biscuits are your thing, Cakehead was the top winner in the 2012 International Biscuit Festival with its signature Cajun Tater savory treat, made with three kinds of bell peppers, garlic, potatoes and corn. Find it in the mornings at the Little River counter. (864) 585-8774, Tues-Fri 9am-5:30pm, Sat 9am-noon. *cakeheadbakeshop.com*

BROADWAY BAGELS | 1200 E. Main St, 29302

This is the best place for New York Style bagels in Spartanburg. They make their bagels fresh every morning for breakfast and continue serving through lunch, where you can also get sandwiches, wraps and salads. The aroma alone of this place is enough to keep you coming back. Hint: arrive early. While the shop makes a variety of bagels (everything from plain to cheddar to the classic everything-bagel), they are busy in the morning and right on through lunch, so get there while the gettin's good. (864) 591-0058, Mon-Fri, 6:30am-2pm, Sat/Sun 7am-2pm.

BLONDIE'S CAFÉ | *2919 Boiling Springs Rd, Boiling Springs, 29316*

This is one of those places that on your first visit you feel like a regular. It could be because you are surrounded by family. Julie, the owner, is in the kitchen along with her daughter. Both her sisters are working the tables. There's a constant stream of talk, and if you start talking smack, you better

hold on because it's coming right back at ya. These tattooed ladies serve up homemade breakfast and lunch in this eclectic house turned restaurant decorated with art by Julie's son, who goes by "Brother." Make sure you save room for a muffin. (864) 474-8400, 7 days a week, 6:30am-3pm.

MON AMIE MORNING CAFÉ | *2601 E. Main St, 29307*

Combine a Southern traditional breakfast with a French vibe. Throw in a European open-air design, a demonstration-style kitchen with a beret-wearing chef, a quaint yellow-and-black décor, and some of the most experienced restaurateurs in Spartanburg. What you get is Mon Amie, serving up crepes, omelets, and exceptional French Toast. Ignore the bowling alley next door—you are dining on the Hub City's Left Bank. Savor breakfast, brunch and lunch there. (864) 541-7981, Wed-Sun 8am-3pm. *monamiemorningcafe.com*

DOLLINE'S | *140 S. Main St, Clifton, 29342*

In a tiny building Dolline Inman serves up an old-school breakfast and lunch in a setting that evokes memories of textile mill life. If you want an authentic treat, come on Wednesday mornings, when a group of old-timers bring their musical instruments for a gospel sing-along.

At lunch you can still get the mill village staples: pinto beans, cornbread, onions and sweet tea, all for less than $5. At breakfast, if you're feeling adventurous, try the livermush. (864) 579-9273, Tues-Sat 7am-2pm.

HEALTH-IN-HAND \ *201-A Wall St, 29306*

Though the store may be small, Health-in-Hand packs a lot into their business. Their main endeavor is juice: you can get yours fresh-pressed while you wait or pick up a pre-pressed bottle, all made with fresh fruits and vegetables. Additionally, there are sweet and savory options for both lunch and breakfast, whether you're in the mood for a wrap, salad or adult fruit cup. The store stocks detox kits, herbal tinctures, salves and kombucha. Browse the Juicing Bible while you wait, unless you've ordered a Hangover Helper—then you might just need to take a seat. (864) 707-2692, Mon-Fri 7:30am-6pm, Sat 9am-4pm. *healthinhandsc.com*

CAFE AROUND THE CORNER \ *121 Dunbar St, 29306*

This sidewalk café offers farm-to-fork fare with surprises on the menu almost every week. Want a black bean-quinoa-kale burger? How about a grilled Atomic Pickle sandwich made with 1,000-day-old Canadian cheddar cheese? This boutique café, with tables inside and outside, is run by Leslie Lattanzio, whose background is as varied as her menu. She's just added Spartanburg's most eclectic tapas-style dinner menu, too.

All together, Café Around the Corner is a treasure chest of healthy eating options. (704) 650-5447, Mon-Fri 11am-3pm. Wed-Fri 5:30-9pm.

Willy Taco delivers on funky atmosphere and delicious grub.

WILLY TACO | *930 E. Main St, 29302*

With an award-winning menu designed by local artist Shannon Kemp and slap full of culinary creativity from chef William Cribb, Willy Taco will impress even the most fastidious foodie. Nothing about this taqueria's cuisine is mainstream. Whether you're in the mood for tacos, tortas or tequila, this joint's Mexican fusion dishes and drinks blend traditional elements with unexpected ingredients. We doubt you've ever seen a taco like the Cumin Crusted Tuna, mixing Mexican spices with Japanese flavors. And don't neglect the Southern Tide, a local favorite with crispy shrimp, pico, and a surprising plot twist, pimento cheese. Willy Taco has plenty of options for ethical eaters as well, from veggie tacos to the Anti Cow tortas with Eric's tree-huggin' tofu.

Willy Taco's atmosphere matches the eclectic, original vibe of the menu. From the patio's reclaimed car seat couch and up-cycled industrial light fixtures, to the Dia de los Muertos paintings imported from Mexico, the décor is just as unique and creative as the food. With playlists even Pitchfork would endorse, Willy Taco always has great tracks to accentuate the lively ambience. There's always a good time at Willy Taco, especially when it's Happy Hour. For discounts on margs, drafts and apps, stop by any afternoon between Tuesday and Friday. Sunday brunch is not to be missed, especially since you can wash it down with a blood orange mimosa. If your crew prefers fresh dishes and fun times, find your way to Willy Taco and get yourselves some. (864) 327-8282, Tues-Thurs 11am-10pm, Fri-Sat 11am-11pm, Sun 10am-9pm. *willytaco.com*

EL MOLCAJETE | *1212 E. Main St, Duncan, 29334*

We're not lacking for Mexican restaurants around here, but El Molcajete stands out among the rest. This restaurant moves beyond the simple Tex-Mex combinations and embraces more traditional Mexican dishes. We can attest that if you're looking for good mole sauce, this is your place. And if you're really brave you can go for the special dish that gives this restaurant its name. Imagine a huge bowl (really a traditional stone cooking utensil) filled with shrimp, chicken, sausage, cactus, in a ranchero sauce and served with generous sides. We recommend making room in your stomach hours in advance. (864) 433-0308, Mon-Thurs 11am-9:30pm, Fri-Sat, 11am-10pm.

EL BURRITO | *3614 Parris Bridge Rd, 29316*

There aren't any other restaurants on the two-lane stretch of asphalt north of Spartanburg where El Burrito can be found. The tiny taqueria itself barely qualifies for the title. With just enough room for four small tables and a counter for ordering, people don't come here for the ambience; they come for the food. El Burrito serves up classic Mexican street food with a sense of authenticity swankier, hipper places just can't match. From the fresh-made tortillas, rolled out by hand and cooked to order, to the delicious homemade hot sauces, El Burrito is a true gem, worth going out of your way to visit. (864) 814-0770, Mon-Thurs 10am-8pm, Fri 10am-5pm, Sun 8am-5pm.

TACO DOG | *1915 E. Main St #7, 29307*

There are taquerias and there are hot dog joints. Never the two shall meet ... except at Taco Dog. The idea of grilled gourmet hot dogs sharing a menu with stuffed burritos, quesadillas, and tacos might seem counterintuitive, but it just plain works. Lines of people stretching to the door during the lunch hours prove it. If you're feeling particularly hungry and adventurous, try a fish taco (grilled tilapia with baja sauce, lettuce and tomatoes) alongside a Carolina dog (mustard, chili and onions) for the full Taco Dog experience. Don't you want a cerveza to go with that? (864) 542-8058, Mon-Sat 11am-9pm. *tacodog.com*

LITTLE RIVER COFFEE BAR | *188 W. Main St, 29306*

Sure, Spartanburg has a Starbucks. What town doesn't have one of those overpriced, sterile, bland coffee-serving corporate catastrophes these days? Those in the know in Spartanburg know better. For locals who care more about what their coffee tastes like than they do about properly pronouncing words like "venti" and "grande," there's Little River Coffee Bar.

Owing to its downtown location, the Coffee Bar serves a veritable who's who of Spartanburg's business and cultural leaders in the mornings, but as afternoon turns to evening, Little River provides a gathering spot for Spartanburg's young creatives, sipping lattes and espresso shots and listening to local musicians on the weekends ranging from avant-garde noise musicians to more traditional folky coffeehouse fare. Be sure to check out

the super-cool mural done by the Hub-Bub artists in residence.

The coffee served by the shop comes from Little River's own roasting company less than a mile and a half away (460 Marion Avenue, (864) 582-7900), an excellent source for gifts to those who appreciate the bean. The roasting company has been locally roasting organic fair trade coffee from Africa and Indonesia, as well as Central and South America since 2002. "It's neat to bring the product that we roast to a place where we can feature it," says Coffee Bar manager Joey Geier. The caffeinated masses of Spartanburg couldn't agree more.

Coffee Bar: (864) 582-1227, Mon-Thur 7am-7pm, Fri/Sat 7am-9pm. *littlerivercoffeebar.com*

Little River Roasting: Mon-Fri 7:30am-4pm. *littleriverroasting.com*

MIYAKO SUSHI GROUP | *116 Magnolia St, 29306*

Another one of downtown's treasures, Miyako Sushi Group (locals affectionately call the place MSG) combines an authentic sushi experience with amazing service and top of the line bartending. Once you get there, after your hot towel has cooled, go ahead and order one of their specialty drinks, maybe even some sake, a Spartanburg roll, a sashimi salad, and then enjoy a nice, relaxed atmosphere. And, once you get done, stick around for a while; they serve up drinks way past dinner time. (864) 583-5112, Lunch: Mon-Fri 11:30am-2pm; Dinner: Mon-Thur 5:30pm-10pm, Fri/Sat 5:30pm-11pm. *miyakosushigroup.com*

DELI KORNER | *1445-A Fernwood-Glendale Rd, 29307*

Run by a German family, Deli Korner has been a staple for more than 30 years and offers a little slice of Deutschland in the heart of the South. Specializing in German and Swiss cuisine, it offers everything from imported sausages (pork and veal), to chocolates filled with liquor. Popular items include the Reuben, Mike's Special (an open-faced Black Forest ham sandwich), and the chef salad with house-made dill dressing. Be sure to try the potato salad, which is light and flavored with bacon and green onions. After eating, you can browse the specialty store, which stocks hard-to-find imports like German beer and baking mixes. On Saturdays when the accordion player stops by, the Frauleins behind the counter are known to break into song. (864) 583-9518, Mon-Fri 10am-5pm; Sat 10am-4pm. *delikorner.com*

CUZINA GRILL | *910 E. Main St, 29302*

Spartanburg has strong Greek connections—a century ago immigrants came looking for Sparta-burg—and because of that we're lucky to have Effie Scordilis and her Cuzina Grill, which serves up freshly made hummus, tabouli, spanakopita, along with a variety of lamb, kefetes (meatball) and falafel plates. One of our favorite dishes (and oh-so-perfect for Spartanburg tastes) is saganaki, or fried cheese. With photos on the walls of the old country, Cuzina is an intimate neighborhood gathering place for an Alfa beer after work or an affordable Mediterranean feast in the late evening. (864) 585-3720, Mon-Thurs 11am-8:30pm, Fri 11am-10pm, Sat noon-10pm.

*Ike's gets crowded for a reason. Don't forget
about the deck out back for additional seating.*

IKE'S KORNER GRILLE \ *104 Archer Rd, 29303*

The contest for the best burger in Spartanburg is a fierce one, with
seemingly every flat-top grill in town having its own contingent of
supporters. In that competition, Ike's Korner Grille may seem like
an underdog. A small restaurant on the outskirts of the Beaumont
mill village, Ike's is an unassuming place on the outside. Walk inside
though, and the crowd tells you everything you need to know.

Every day without fail, there's a motley group of business people, retirees,
and blue-collar workers gathered around the bar and crowded around the
tables for what they argue is the best burger in town. However you order
it, you can be sure that this fresh, hand-pattied burger, (served with the
excellent hand-cut fries by a cook who goes by "Fry Daddy") will be delicious.

Regulars also rave about the bologna sandwich, a thick hand-cut slice
grilled or "burnt," and served on a hamburger bun. For the particularly
adventurous, Ike's also has a "Wall of Fame Burger." The monstrous
sandwich features four burger patties, two slices of bologna, 12 to 16
slices of bacon, six to eight slices of cheese, two eggs, and basically every
topping in the house. Finish the burger with a side of french fries, onion
rings, and a drink, and you'll get a T-shirt and your picture immortalized
on Ike's wall. (864) 542-0911, Mon–Fri 10am–9pm, Sat 7am–3pm.

THE SKILLET \ 435 E. Main St, 29302

This cozy little dive has been a mainstay of Spartanburg breakfast dining for more than 50 years, so plan on a wait if you come Saturday morning. About the size of a standard living room, the Skillet has a half dozen tables and two counter sections with stools—come for the "counter culture" says one regular—where you can watch the line cooks grilling the food you just ordered. Try the biscuits and sausage gravy and wash it down with endless cups of coffee. Be sure not to miss the portrait of Gen. Robert E. Lee. (864) 342-9978, Mon-Sat 6am-2pm, Sun 8am-2pm. *theskilletspartanburg.com*

SIMPLE SIMON \ 109 S. Pine St, 29302

As evidenced by the classic sign out front, Simple Simon is retro all the way. This is an old-school diner known for apple butter pancakes, crunchy French toast, liver mush, eggs, grits and bacon in the morning, and—as we say in the South—meat-and-three the rest of the day. There's good conversation at the counter, and be sure to pay a visit to the party room, festooned with Elvis and Marilyn Monroe memorabilia and more. (864) 585-8844, open 18 hours a day—all morning and all night, but closed from 2pm-9pm.

PAPA'S BREAKFAST NOOK \ 191 E. Saint John St, 29306

Where do you get a plate of food in this town after midnight? Papa's Breakfast Nook is a late-night institution among Spartanburg's college bar-hopping set, and in a city known for housing Denny's corporate headquarters, that's saying something. The late-night crowd at this 24-hour greasy spoon and breakfast diner is generally split over burgers or breakfast, but the smart money at Papa's is on the omelets, especially the famous "trashcan" omelet featuring ham, American and Swiss cheeses, bacon, onions, green peppers, tomatoes and mushrooms. (864) 582-6655, open 24/7. *papasbreakfastnook.com*

did you know?

FOOD A-PLENTY

The Beacon Drive-In is hardly "underground," but a Spartanburg guidebook without the world-renowned drive-in is like an onion ring ... well, without the grease. Roadfood.com called it "the most intense restaurant you'll ever visit." The Food Network and CBS' "60 Minutes" have been there, as well as presidential candidates galore. The Beacon claims to sell more onions and more sweet tea than any restaurant in America. Visit the chili-cheese capital of the world at 255 John B. White Blvd. (864) 585-9387, Mon-Thu 6:30am-9:30pm, Fri & Sat 6:30am-10pm, Sun 11am-8pm. beacondrivein.com

TNT HOTWINGS

456 Union St, 29306

In an unassuming building that once housed a KFC (back when it was called Kentucky Fried Chicken) is a place with a treasure trove of amazing flavors. The fires that they ignite on tongues have gained quite a reputation. Warning: An upset stomach is imminent for those brave enough to try the Atomic Blast sauce. (864) 585-9996, Mon-Tues 5-10pm, Wed-Thurs 11am-2pm/5pm-11:30pm, Fri 11am-11:30pm, Sat 11am-1:30am. *tnthotwings.com*

GRILLE 221

4795 S. Church St Ext #10, 29376

"Best burgers on the Highway," proclaims the menu at Grille 221 and though there might not be a lot of competition around these parts to dispute the claim, the place still serves up some great food. Burgers and canned beer are the order of the day, but the real treat is the crowd. This is a regular gathering spot for locals discussing everything from various caliber hunting rifles to who's going to win next week's NASCAR race. Grille 221 is as authentic a working class restaurant and watering hole as you're ever likely to find. (864) 595-1178, Mon-Wed 11am-10pm, Thurs-Sat 11am-until.

THE BARN GRILL AND BAR | *1441 Union St, 29302*

If you like burgers and hand-cut fries, this place is in the running for some of the best in town, though you wouldn't tell it from the outside. This 50-year-old building was recently purchased by a local couple who have added the Grill in the back. You'll find lots of handmade items on the menu, like their chicken salad and pimento cheese. Our suggestion is to try the Big Moo. On the bar side, there are some pool tables, TVs, video games and all their beer comes in cans. Because it sits in the county, you can smoke in the bar. (864) 707-5068, Mon-Sat 11am-8pm for the Grill, later for the Bar.

UNITED HOUSE OF PRAYER FOR ALL PEOPLE . *660 S. Church St, 29306*

It's a church, of course, but it's also a great place to grab a delicious homemade lunch or early dinner. Look, this is no-frills. You enter into a cafeteria, but this isn't school-food fakery: on any given day there's homemade fried chicken, roasted chicken, meatloaf, ribs, pork loin—even chitlins'—and plenty of sides, usually including mac 'n' cheese, potato salad, cornbread, rolls, rice and gravy, collard greens and other veggies. Be sure to check out their own sweet tea and lemonade, as well.

Amid portraits of Daddy Grace and TVs showing Andy Griffith reruns, grab a seat at a long table and strike up a conversation. You and your fellow diners won't be strangers for long. This is no nonsense, home-cooked goodness—the fried chicken is crisp on the outside, tender and juicy on the inside and perfectly spiced. The meatloaf is light and tasty. Another bit of advice: come hungry. While the meals are inexpensive (between $6-8), the plates are large and your eyes can easily be a bit too overzealous. This is what community is all about: a church making good quality yet inexpensive meals for the people. There's every reason to support such a place and to enjoy the food while you do. (864) 585-2673, Mon-Fri 11am-3pm, Sat & Sun noon-5pm.

*Amazing, authentic food
served up by the saucy-talking owner
makes this place one that we love.*

A CARIBBEAN SWEETNESS | *1824 E. Main St, 29307*

Cuban native Gaston Rodriguez opened this restaurant in 2008 after friends and family raved about his Cuban sandwiches, coffee and Caribbean milkshakes made with fruit and sweetened condensed milk. The Cuban sandwich is divine, and daily special plates pair meats like Salsa Chicken and Barbacoa Beef with sides like roasted plantains, yellow rice and tamales. Seating inside the restaurant, part of what was once a house, is limited, but during the warmer months the best seats are outside on the large patio. Often, meals are served by Rodriguez himself, who enjoys bantering back and forth with customers, telling stories about his childhood in Cuba. "People tell me coming here is like coming over to a friend's house. To me, that's the highest compliment you can pay," says Rodriguez. (864) 582-3330, Tues-Sat noon-9pm.

did you know?

HUB CITY DELIVERY

Your favorite restaurant doesn't deliver? Problem solved! This delivery service will bring orders from nearly three dozen restaurants—plus a florist—to you. Plan to pay a modest delivery charge and tip your driver (because that's how they get paid) plus the cost of your grub. (864) 909-3793, Mon-Thur 11am-2pm, 4:30-9pm; Fri 11am-2pm, 4:30-10pm; Sat noon-10pm; Sun noon-9pm. *hubcitydelivery.com*

THAI FOOD

Downtown Spartanburg offers two amazing Thai eateries. Monsoon Noodle House has become a favorite—especially with college students. With a wide variety of appetizers, noodle bowls and stir-fry dishes, there's something for everyone. Service is unbelievably fast, perfect for takeout or a quick dinner date. If it's a fancy date or you've got time to linger, try Lime Leaf down the street. It features fine appetizers, curry and noodle dishes, and tasty desserts such as bananas

covered in coconut and deep fried with chocolate sauce. The striking and intimate décor was designed by owner Kanas Lam, who also decorated several other restaurant interiors, including Monsoon Noodle House. Just outside downtown, Bangkok Thai Café also offers staple dishes such as curry and pad Thai, as well as specialties. There's a second iteration—Bangkok 2—in Boiling Springs. On the west side, Thai Taste on Southport Road offers an extensive menu in a casual dining setting. No matter where you are in Spartanburg, it's likely you're not terribly far from a bowl of great noodles.

Monsoon Noodle House
129 W. Main St, 29306
(864) 582-0618
Mon-Thur: 11am-3pm, 5-9:30pm
Fri: 11am-3pm, 5-10:30pm
Sat: noon-3pm, 5-10:30pm
Sun: noon-3pm, 5-9:30pm

Bangkok Thai Café
1200 E. Main St #16
(864) 583-2532
Sun-Thur: 11am-3, 5-9:30pm
Fri: 11am-3, 5-10:30pm
Sat: 4-10:30pm
Closed Monday

Lime Leaf
101 E. Main St
(864) 542-2171
Mon-Thur: 11:30am-2:30pm, 5-10pm
Fri: 11:30am-2:30pm, 5-10:30pm
Sat: 5-10:30pm
Sun: 5-9pm

Thai Taste
145 Southport Rd
(864) 595-6040
Mon-Thur: 11am-9:30pm
Fri: 11am-10pm
Sat: noon-10pm
Closed Sunday

FARMERS' MARKETS AND MONARCH CAFÉ

498 Howard St, 29303

Spartanburg has a swanky new farmers' market at **Northside Harvest Park**, open on Saturdays 8am-noon, nine months a year, with an on-site café, a working farm and a B-cycle station. Trust us, you don't need to be anywhere else on a Saturday morning. While most of the 25+ vendors are selling fruits and veggies, you can also find Little River coffee, products from Those Pickle Ladies, Blue Moon Specialty Foods' pimento cheeses and great sauces (we highly recommend the Voodoo Chutney), local eggs and beef, and a variety of homemade crafts such as soaps, candles and bowls. And in the summer ... peaches, galore! *hubcityfm.org*

Monarch Café and Fresh Food Store is operated by the Butterfly Foundation (butterflysc.org), which trains economically challenged individuals for careers in food service. They mostly cook from locally grown and organic food. The fried fish and grits are phenomenal. And where else in town can you get deviled eggs? Open weekdays 8-5 and during market.

The Hub City Farmers Market also operates in the summer on Wall Street (just off Morgan Square) on Wednesdays from 11am-1pm. And if you're up for a whole farmers' market tour, well, you're in luck—there are two others. **The Cowpens Farmers Market**, located inside a very cool former hardware supply house on S. Main St., is open Feb-Dec, 10-3 p.m. and has local artisans in addition to farmers. **The Landrum Farmers Market** is open at 111 N. Trade St., May-Oct, 7-11am. This is where you hook up with C-Saw Hill, producers of local grass-fed beef and pasture-raised pork and chicken. Make it a day and try all of them.

JOHN SMITH HILL FARM | *199 Dobson Heights Rd, 29307*

This Clifton farm may be named after a man, but it's a woman who makes this eco-friendly operation tick. Syglenda Saziru will eagerly tell you about the farm's newest endeavor—whether it's goat-milk soaps, butter or scented oils—because it seems like the Farm is always up to something new. And after you have learned more about the woman behind John Smith Hill, grab some eggs because they will change your life. (864) 497-3271, Mon-Sun by appointment. *johnsmithhill.com*

ABBOTT FARMS | *4 Spartanburg locations, 1 Gaffney location*

Looking for a taste of SC? Abbott Farms has got you covered. They have tree-ripened peaches from mid-May to mid-September along with watermelons, cantaloupes, peanuts (boiled & roasted) and a huge selection of jams, jellies, pickles, salsas, hot sauces and honey. Wash it all down with a Nehi or Cheerwine and a check out their huge selection of fireworks in every store. And ... they ship! (Sorry, can't do the fireworks). Check their website for seasonal hours. (800) 764-0076. *abbottfarmsonline.com*

STRAWBERRY HILL U.S.A | *3097 Hwy 11 West, Chesnee, 29323*

This a tourist trap that locals love. The Chesnee produce stand and farm store is a strawberry mecca in April and May when strawberries are in season, and one of the biggest peach-picking operations in the South during the summer. Don't miss their ice cream stand and café where you can indulge in some fresh and gravy-soaked Southern cuisine. And make your way through the 10-acre Corn Maze every October. (864) 461-7225, 8am-8pm April 15 thru Nov. 1. *strawberryhillusa.com*

NIVENS APPLE FARM | *130 Orchard Dr, 29369*

Come for the juicy apples but stay for a theme park of farm-life fun. At Nivens there's plenty to do besides pick apples (or choose a pumpkin in season). First of all, there's Wilbur the Pig. And don't miss the sprawling State of South Carolina Corn Maze! There's a hayride, a Storybook Character Trail, a gem mine and pedal cars. And for those who just want to eat, there's a great farm store. (864) 574-8889. Opens mid-Aug, Mon-Sat 8am-6pm; Sun 1-6pm. *nivensapplefarm.com*

THE HARE AND HOUND PUB \ *101 E. Rutherford St, Landrum, 29356*

This is a haven for a civilized pint after wandering the wilds where
Spartanburg County meets North Carolina. The wood-warmed, horse-
enthused pub caters to a mixed crowd of longtime locals, new arrivals
discussing house plans with their architects and the always gregarious
equestrian set. Admire the creamy brown head on your draft Guinness
and partake of traditional pub fare like Chicken Pot Pie or the day's
freshly baked quiche. For dinner have Rick's Famous BBQ Baby Back
Ribs (Friday and Saturday only) when you feel like a good ol' boy at
heart. (864) 457-3232, 11am-10pm every day. *thehareandhound.com*

STONE SOUP \ *1522 E. Rutherford St, Landrum, 29356*

This place says cozy and calm from the moment you walk in the door. Think of
Sunday dinner at your favorite aunt's house, then make her a bit adventurous
with an Asian Shrimp Salad or Spring Pea Ravioli, and an equestrienne for
good measure, and you've got the idea. The soothing atmosphere is perfect
for a leisurely lunch or dinner, either indoors amid the bookshelves and
photographs of local equestrian triumphs or outdoors on the covered patio.
Toast the good life and memories of that eccentric aunt from the full wine and
beer offerings. Life is good. (864) 457-5255, Lunch: Wed-Fri 11:30am-2:30pm;
Dinner, Tues-Sat 5-9pm, Sat/Sun brunch 11am-2pm. *stonesoupoflandrum.com*

did you know?

HUB CITY CO-OP GROCERY   *176 N. Liberty St, 29306*

Spartanburg's Co-op Grocery store is poised to open in early 2016 as the first
consumer retail grocery cooperative in South Carolina. Located across from
the Chapman Cultural Center in a former Volkswagen car dealership, the co-op
will offer fresh produce, dry goods, general grocery items, personal care, bulk
items, cleaning, pre-packaged meats and seafood items, dairy products, baked
goods, health supplements, a deli, prepared grab-and-go-items, a salad bar,
hot bar, candies and beer/wine. Many of these items will come from farms
in the area. Members who pay a one-time fee $150 fee will get lots of fun
benefits, but ownership not required to shop at the store. *hubcitycoop.org*

There's a history lesson imbedded in this mural. Show some love to the 864!

HUB-BUB | *100 S. Spring St, 29306*

Like the cast of "Saturday Night Live," this evolving arts outfit has been the crazy, creative heart of Spartanburg for more than a decade. Lately they've been known for their live late-night talk show, "The Latest Thing in Spartanburg," featuring a hilarious cast and crew of local writers and actors that keep the Sparkle City up-to-date through interviews and sketch comedy. From downtown murals and wacky videos to giant water slides and mini-golf, HUB-BUB's fingerprints are all over this town, and there's really no predicting where they will pop up next. They have a new office right next to the Love Where You Live mural. Check the website to see what the HUB-BUB is all about. (864) 582-0056. *hub-bub.com*

CAROLINA SCULPTURE STUDIO | *193 Twin Creek, 29316*

Set amongst a simple two-acre homestead with gardens, vineyards and pastured chickens is the granite sculpture studio of AC Button II, who continues a 120-year Button family tradition in stonecutting. "There are less than two dozen granite sculptors and even fewer studios left," says Button, whose works are installed across America. "This is a responsibility." Visitors are welcome, but call ahead. Studio time and instructional workshops, for individuals or groups, can be scheduled. (864) 814-6418, by appointment. *carolinasculpturestudio.com*

WEST MAIN ARTISTS CO-OP | *578 W. Main St, 29301*

It may still look like a church on the outside, but inside—in the former Sunday School rooms, the choir rooms and the sanctuary—there's a whole lot of art going on. In fact, this is one of the largest artist co-ops in the whole region, with 34 resident studios that throw their doors open four days a week so the public can come see art in progress and even do a little shopping.

The co-op is the dream of Howard Solomon, an east Texan Air Force pilot and artist who moved to town a few years back and bought the old Baptist Church in foreclosure. An army of local artists swarmed in and, with plenty of sweat equity, ripped out, rebuilt, re-lit and repainted the entire 20,000-square-foot structure.

Members of the West Main Co-op range from outsider-artists to traditionalists: potters, jewelry-makers, painters, printmakers, ceramicists, glass artists, woodworkers and photographers, ranging in age from 20 to 80. There are three exhibition galleries as well as a retail shop where you can find original artwork priced from $15 to $2,000. The real jewel is in the basement where Bill Wheatley runs a 100-year-old letterpress where you can make vintage posters. Visit the website to find out about art classes, music lessons, figure drawing sessions and more. (864) 804-6501, Gallery Shop hours: Tues-Fri 10am-6pm, Sat 10am-4pm, and the third Thursday of the month during Art Walk, 5-9pm. *westmainartists.org*

SPOKEN WORD SPARTANBURG

Spoken Word Spartanburg has grown from an open mic to a multifaceted organization, but it remains dedicated to "the raw, uncut performance art of spoken word and slam poetry." Started by Marlanda Dekine and Antonio Mack, Spoken Word Spartanburg originally held open mic events in Greenville, a lively center of slam poetry. But both founders lived in Spartanburg and wanted to host more events for local residents. They began to bring in out-of-state poets to perform at events and help attract participants. After launching a successful Indiegogo campaign that raised $1,000 dollars,

the group was able to expand its programs, and soon organized the Build-A-Library Book Drive, which donated 2,000 books to kids and held writing workshops with them.

From there, Spoken Word Spartanburg began to solidify its mission of art and activism. Their goal was to build an organization that used spoken word to address issues of inequality and social justice. They now put on a variety of events, including monthly open mics, workshops with visiting artists, and large-scale poetry slams with cash prizes. (Check the web page for times and places.) For the last year and a half, the organization has also held monthly conversations at First Presbyterian Church (393 E. Main St), focused on important topics like "Media, Race, and Perceptions" and "Mental Illness, Suicide, and Race." Anyone can attend these events, and those who choose to become paying members of Spoken Word Spartanburg receive free entry for a year, as well as free admission to workshops. *spokenwordspartanburg.com*

ART WALK | *Downtown and Beyond*

It's free, cultured and often comes with wine and cheese. So put on some comfy shoes, grab a friend and hit the streets every third Thursday of the month as almost a dozen galleries host their monthly open houses. You'll find a diverse mix: from the eclectic assortment at the West Main Artists Co-op, to the high-brow offerings of TJC Gallery, to the occasional pop-up event in an empty storefront, to the "performance art experiment" of Wet Paint Syndrome at the back of Hillcrest Shopping Center, there's something for everyone. (864) 583-2776, third Thursday of the month 5–9pm.

TRAINS ON THE TRAIL |

Access: 325 E. Henry St, 29302; 180 Country Club Rd, 29302

Trains gave Spartanburg the name "Hub City," and now you can take a walk on the Rail Trail to see five funky bronze sculptures of the various cars that rode the local rails in years past: a switcher car, tram, streetcar, caboose and steam engine. Created in 2011 by artist Richard Conn, the sculptures are set on reworked pieces of iron railroad ties. The five sculptures form a children's scavenger hunt with clues available on either end of the trail.

did you know?

ARTISTS-IN-RESIDENCE Spartanburg hosts two cutting-edge artist-in-residence programs that bring emerging filmmakers, theater artists, painters, sculptors, poets and fiction writers to the city from all over the nation to "live free and create."

The HUB-BUB artists-in-residence program, which started in 2006, selects four young creatives to live in a cluster of downtown apartments, January-June. Their influence and art can be found across Spartanburg, from the mural in the Little River Coffee Bar to a memorial on the Pacolet River for the victims of a 1903 flood. They often put in volunteer hours helping local kids make art and film. (864) 582-0056. *hub-bub.com*

Additionally, the Hub City Writers Project operates the Writers House, a downtown bungalow that annually hosts three residencies—spring, summer and fall—for early-career writers. These residents run literary programs, workshops and summer camps for locals. You can often find them working at the Hub City Bookshop. (864) 577-9349. *hubcity.org*

MURAL, MURAL ON THE WALL

Spartanburg suddenly has become a community of murals and graffiti walls. These are not your ordinary tags, haphazardly scribbled on road signs and overpasses, done in the name of vanity and rebellion. No, these are carefully plotted portraits, patterns and phrases—they belong to artists who have chosen to publicly share their identities in colorful and complex arrangements.

The "Love Where You Live" mural, which splashes across the corner of West Main and Spring streets downtown, is based on the famous 6th Street Mural in Austin, Texas. People take wedding pictures there and visitors love it.

Perhaps the most impressive wall is "Beyond Civilization" at 149 S. Daniel Morgan Ave. Commissioned by the alternative arts group HUB-BUB, this one is, in short, breathtaking. As you can tell from the mural, artist Ishmael wants you to read Daniel Quinn's novel Ishmael, a musing on modern civilization. On either side of the mural there exists free space for anyone to come and make art of their own—bring a can of spray paint and make your own mark on Spartanburg.

From there, turn around and see the "Bananas Y'all" mural on the back of a brick garbage shelter. And at Cribb's be sure to check out the giant orange painting that celebrates the brewers' hops and bicycles. Don't miss the "Call It" mural that pays tribute to Beacon Drive-in legend J.C. Stroble over by the Hot Spot Skate Park on Union Street or the work of homegrown celebrity artist Lee Wilke just across the road.

Yes, that's the largest syringe you've ever seen.

MONUMENTAL SCULPTURE GARDEN

800 University Way, 29303

Walking across the vast, green campus of USC Upstate, you might think you've wandered into the movie set for one of the Transformers films. This is the college's Monumental Sculpture Garden, which features modernist pieces of all kinds, some that tower eighteen feet high, others with moving parts, bright colors, or sharp edges. Of particular note is local sculptor Winton Wingo's Gun Amnesty Memorial created with dismantled weapons from the mean streets of Spartanburg. There's also a lime green, blimp-like syringe created by native son Adam Walls. Step in—like it was a rocket ship—and maybe you won't be so spooked at the physician's office next time (at least that's what the sculptor has in mind.)

There are more than 20 pieces installed now, a virtual toy box of giant wedges, cylinders and disks, with plans to add more pieces in the future. Among the featured artists are Mayo Mac Boggs, Bob Doster, Daingerfield Ashton and Mike Williams. *The Monumental Sculpture Garden* is the brainchild of Jane Nodine, a Spartanburg-born abstract artist who has been named as one of the one hundred most significant artists in South Carolina in the 20th century. Visit the college web page, type "monumental" into the search box, and download a PDF to start your tour. Be sure to bring your cell phone to get the audio tour. (864) 503-5000, everyday during daylight hours. *uscupstate.edu*

GALLERY EAST \ *512 E. Main St, 29302*

Gallery owner Jason Hiltabiddle took a break from his life as a general contractor to open a stunning new gallery exhibiting the work of contemporary and pop artists from the Upstate and beyond. The remodeled interior of this 1930s-era grocery is as striking as the artwork inside. The gallery features rotating shows and relatively low-priced art. (864) 804-6067, open for special events and during Art Walk every third Thursday, 6-9pm. *thegalleryeast.com*

THE ART LOUNGE \ *500 E. Main St, 29302*

This converted gas station is a showcase of Spartanburg's art. Brandi Dice, the incredibly personable owner, says, "Ninety-eight percent of everything in here is from Spartanburg-based artists, and with the exception of a few prints these are all original, one-of-a-kind pieces." You'll find paintings, jewelry and sculpture from folks who've been with her since she opened shop in 2011.

Beyond their gallery display, The Art Lounge offers a variety of events for art enthusiasts. Outdoor Art Markets happen on a Saturday in April and September and are open to any local artist to display. It's a chance to pick up emerging artists' pieces at a great price. Then there are the Wine & Paint nights that happen quarterly. Led by a local artist, you pay your money, show up and everything is provided—canvases, brushes, paint and, of course, wine. Definitely stop in during Art Walk. You may find musicians playing, a beer tasting or live painting.

If you need something framed, like a revolver, a jacket, an award or a movie poster, they can handle it. The Art Lounge boasts the most samples of frames of anyone in town. (864) 804-6566, Mon-Thur 10am-5pm, Fri 10am-4pm, Sat. by appt., during third Thursday Art Walks, 6-9pm, and occasional night events. *artlounge1.com*

UPSTATE GALLERY ON MAIN | *172 E. Main St, 29306*

Who knew you could see iconic work by Andy Warhol in a small gallery on Spartanburg's Main Street? The art faculty and students of the University of South Carolina Upstate run this "experiential gallery" called UGOM, which focuses on modern, out-of-the box works. You can see Warhol prints and photos, plus examples of the cameras he used. You can also drop in and watch students hang the shows. Every six to eight weeks a new show goes up, spotlighting artists from the college's permanent collection. (864) 503-5689, Tues-Sat noon-5pm (no Saturdays in the summer) and during Art Walk nights.

TJC GALLERY | *154 W. Main St, 29306*

Located in a beautiful old building in Morgan Square, TJC Gallery rotates exhibitions featuring works of art from the Johnson Collection—a privately owned collection of paintings reflecting the history and culture of the American South. The Johnson Collection includes the work of hundreds of artists, with pieces from the 1700s to the present. (864) 594-5864, Tues & Thurs 1-5pm and during Art Walk every third Thursday, 6-9pm. *thejohnsoncollection.org*

CAROLINA GALLERY | *523 W. Main St, 29301*

You may think you're in a small town, but this is a big-city gallery experience. Representing numerous local and regional artists, owner Ed Emory says it's not unusual for visitors to admire a piece, meet the artist, and become fast friends. They offer professional fine art framing along with Giclee printing. Ed throws a great party during Artwalk, too. (864) 585-3335 Tues-Fri 10:30am-5pm, Sat 11am-4pm. *carolinagalleryart.com*

H + K GALLERY | *151 W. Main St, 29306*

Incredible art deco doors are your first signal that H + K is a high-class joint, filled with fine art from across the South. But when the weather is nice, owner Susan Kunkler and her daughter, Claire, throw open those big, fancy doors to the public and are waiting at the threshold for visitors to chat with. There's some true Southern hospitality in this place. Come in for a quick lesson in Charleston Renaissance art and its contemporary cousins. Be sure to check out the funky spiral staircase. (864) 345-2262, Tues-Sat 11am-4pm and during Art Walk nights. *handkgallery.com*

LIBRARY EXHIBITIONS \ *151 S. Church St, 29306*

The library in this town really does it all, and lately the downtown headquarters has been getting into the art show business. Head down the big staircase into the AT&T Exhibition Lobby (sorry, no old phones on display) to catch the annual Collegiate Invitational Art Exhibition in the spring and the annual Juried Exhibition of local artists in the fall. When there's not art on the wall, there are some pretty cool exhibits focusing on social issues and traveling displays from the S.C. State Museum. (864) 596-3500 Mon-Fri 9am-9pm, Sat 9am-6pm, Sun 1:30-6pm. *infodepot.org*

SPARTANBURG ART MUSEUM \ *200 E. St. John St, 29306*

This is not your average art museum. The Spartanburg Art Museum (SAM) serves the community through its ever changing exhibitions, the Art School, and COLORS, an after-school outreach program for underserved youth living in Spartanburg County. This cultural institution is located at the Chapman Cultural Center and serves thousands of art lovers, learners

and doers annually. Exhibitions rotate on average every three months and have included solo and group shows, site-specific installations and community exhibitions featuring the work of regional artists. The most popular exhibition in 2014, Memory Ship by Christopher Nitsche, was an installation of a ship form using over 500 square feet of salvaged lumber that appeared to bisect gallery walls. Inside the ship were thousands of found objects arranged to express the artist's ideas and associations of memory. SAM has a funky vibe these days and is worth checking out. (864) 582-7616, Tues-Sat 10am-5pm, Sundays 1-5pm, or on the third Thursday evening of each month during ArtWalk. *spartanburgartmuseum.org*

CAROLINA FOOTHILLS ARTISAN CENTER

124 W. Cherokee St, Chesnee, 29323
214 E. Rutherford St, Landrum, 29356

If you're shopping for regional arts and crafts, your best strategy may be to venture out into the smaller towns north of Spartanburg. That's where you'll find two galleries operated by the not-for-profit Carolina Foothills Artisan Center. Established in 2000 to showcase emerging and established artists and craftsmen from the two Carolinas, CFAC operates its original gallery in downtown Chesnee, and now has a second location in the heart of Landrum. Both locations are well worth a visit.

What is most appealing about CFAC is the mixture of art and craft found here. Expertly turned (and reasonably priced) wooden bowls, lovely blown and slumped glass objects, handmade jewelry, and functional pottery are pleasantly displayed alongside funky anthropomorphic portraits, traditional oil and watercolor landscapes, and photography.

If whimsy and repurposed items are your thing, look no further. Delicate shotgun shell jewelry, farm implement sculpture and up-cycled furniture abound. In short, you're just as likely to discover works by visionary self-taught artists as you are fine craft, so this is a great place for browsing or finding one-of-a-kind wedding gifts.

Each month CFAC spotlights one artist with an exhibit and opening reception, details of which can be found on their Facebook page. And since arts education is central to its mission, classes and workshops for children and adults are offered weekly.

Caveat emptor: the town of Chesnee frowns upon speeding drivers.

Don't ask how we know. You've been warned.

Chesnee (864) 461-3050; Landrum (864) 457-1189. Landrum: Mon 10:30am-2:30pm Both: Thurs-Sat 10:30am-5pm, First Fridays in Landrum until 8pm.

Let your inner artist out! Who knows, you might be a genius.

MAKE YOUR OWN

After touring Spartanburg's galleries and public sculpture, don't be surprised if you feel like getting artsy yourself. Spartanburg has two great paint-your-own establishments; you don't need to bring anything but your own artistic vision. For over 15 years, **Hearts of Clay**—previously known as Flying Saucers—has been Spartanburg's premiere paint-your-own pottery studio at 660 Spartan Blvd. Whether it's a commemorative tile, a penguin figurine, a decorative plate, picture frames or piggy banks, Hearts of Clay provides a huge selection of blank pieces waiting to be personalized. Once you've finished, the staff will fire the piece in one of their four kilns and you can take it home a week later. In addition to pottery painting, you can create your own clay sculpture or glass fusion jewelry. Whether you're a master ceramicist or tot-sized finger-painter, Hearts of Clay has a geegaw for you. (864) 576-2228. *heartsofclay.com*

If you work better in two dimensions rather than three, downtown's **East Main Arts** at 167 E. Main St. has everything an aspiring Van Gogh could need. Pre-sketched canvases are available or take your chance with freehand sketching. Send in a photo of your beloved pet ahead of time, buy a bottle of wine and get ready to make a masterpiece. If you're more of a free spirit, there are also open studios for experimentation. (864) 430-1040. *eastmainarts.com*

Both spots offer birthday parties, specializing in princess themes with cameos from local Elsas, Rapunzels and post-mermaid Ariels. For grown-ups, you can book either spot for a bachelorette party or ladies' brunch.

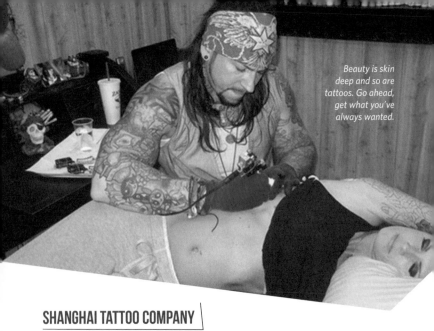

Beauty is skin deep and so are tattoos. Go ahead, get what you've always wanted.

SHANGHAI TATTOO COMPANY

8031 Warren H Abernathy Hwy, 29301

If you want to get a great tattoo in Spartanburg, look no further than Shanghai Tattoo. Hidden away in a tiny strip mall on the west side of town, Shanghai has become a haven for those who might be wary of tattoo shops. Since tattooing has only recently been made legal in the state, it can be difficult to find an artist with enough skill and experience to design a great custom piece. Owner Jason "Thumper" Lightfoot, a former marine who bears an uncanny resemblance to Captain Jack Sparrow, brought his shop to Spartanburg for just that reason: "I figured you bring 19 years of experience to a place where it's a relatively new environment, you're going to bring something to the area that people haven't seen before," he says. Jason and his staff are honest, professional and talented. The shop is impeccably clean and the staff is super friendly. (864) 574-8282, Tues-Thurs noon-8pm, Fri-Sat, noon-10pm. *shanghaitattoocompany.com*

Shanghai isn't the only tattoo game in town though. Others include: **Sparkle City Tattoos** (2811 Reidville Road, (864) 327-8371), **Tattoo Wearhouse** (740 Oak Grove Rd, (864) 576-8552), **Lucky Dice Tattoos** (412 W. Blackstock Rd, (864) 804-6052), **Darkside Custom Tattoo** (2313 Reidville Rd, (864) 595-7231), **Palmetto Ink** (1517 Asheville Hwy, (864) 327-5092), **Chastain Tattoo** (7119 Lone Oak Rd, (864) 357-0892) and **Twisted Needle Tattoo & Piercing** (1791 E. Blackstock Rd (864) 576-0750).

THEATRE ON CAMPUS

From Shakespeare to Sondheim, Williams to Wilde, the college theatre scene in Spartanburg is shaking things up with shows that are provocative, powerful and passionate. Theatre/Converse, Wofford Theatre and the Shoestring Players of USC Upstate are making the old new again while pushing the boundaries of the modern theatre with performances by students, faculty, professionals and members of the surrounding community.

Big musicals are your thing? *Cabaret, Gypsy, Urinetown* and *Legally Blonde* all have been performed on the college stage in Spartanburg. Modern classics more your style? *Red, Very Still and Hard to See, Arcadia* and *How I Learned to Drive* have also been staged. Original works, perhaps? *The Anointing of Dracula, 7 Plays for Evil People* and *One Hour with 3 Lepers*!

Featuring six venues between the three schools—from the intimate Tony White theatre at Wofford, to the Performing Arts Center at Upstate and the historic Hazel Abbott Theatre at Converse—these programs offer more than twenty productions each year with ticket prices about the cost of a movie ticket. Now there are even more reasons to spend an evening in the dark. So check out what's playing and get to Converse, Wofford and Upstate. There's always something going onstage.

converse.edu, (864) 596-9068
wofford.edu, (864) 597-4080
uscupstate.edu, (864) 503-5695

PLAYHAUS

Every Monday night, a group of friendly artists, friends and beer lovers gather at Growler Haus (113 N. Church St. 29306) to drink from the best beer menu in town and share new work for the screen and stage. What began as a group of actors and writers who were passionate about new work has grown into a supportive group of lovers of stories of all sorts. Anyone is welcome to come listen, read or share their own new works in a supportive atmosphere with constructive feedback. Grab a pint (or flight) and fall down a rabbit hole of storytelling. Mondays, 7:30pm.

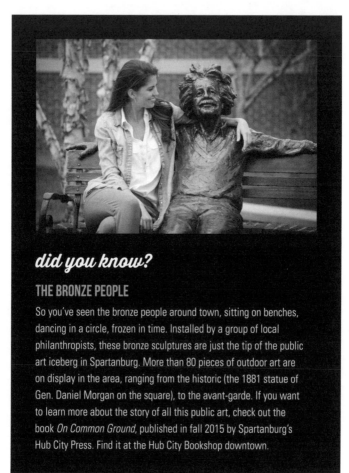

did you know?

THE BRONZE PEOPLE

So you've seen the bronze people around town, sitting on benches, dancing in a circle, frozen in time. Installed by a group of local philanthropists, these bronze sculptures are just the tip of the public art iceberg in Spartanburg. More than 80 pieces of outdoor art are on display in the area, ranging from the historic (the 1881 statue of Gen. Daniel Morgan on the square), to the avant-garde. If you want to learn more about the story of all this public art, check out the book *On Common Ground*, published in fall 2015 by Spartanburg's Hub City Press. Find it at the Hub City Bookshop downtown.

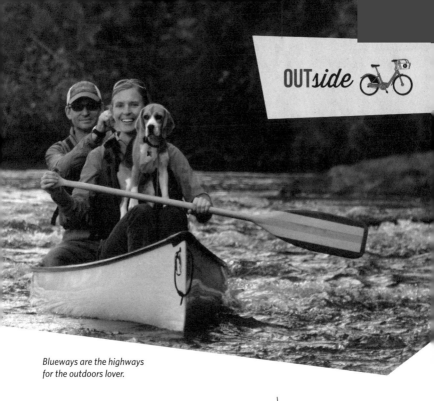

*Blueways are the highways
for the outdoors lover.*

PACOLET RIVER HERITAGE TRUST PRESERVE \ *Lucky Lane, 29302*

Nine miles east of Spartanburg, this preserve has a quiet and easy 1.5 mile out-and-back hike down to the Pacolet River, through woods inhabited by ancients. The 270-acre preserve is dotted with soapstone outcroppings that were carved into bowls thousands of years ago. It is also home to an alien-looking prehistoric "glyph" in an undisclosed location. Can you find it? The soapstone is a tangible link to our distant past, so please do not disturb it. (864) 948-0000, dawn to dusk daily. *spartanburgconservation.org*

GLENN SPRINGS PASSAGE OF THE PALMETTO TRAIL \

Rolling farmlands, mature forests of oak and hickory and the historic town of Glenn Springs highlight this 7-mile passage of the mountains-to-the-sea statewide trail. As the former site of a popular 1800s resort hotel, the Glenn Springs historic district includes 20 buildings—homes, churches, and ruins—within its 90 acres. Park near the historic post office (SC Hwy 150 and Boys Home Road), the midway point of this trail, and you can walk north or south. *palmettotrail.org/GlennSprings.asp*

Over 100 acres of greenspace within the city limits. Fido will love this!

COTTONWOOD TRAIL | *479 Beechwood Dr, 29307*

Five minutes from downtown, the Cottonwood Trail in the Edwin Griffin Preserve gives runners, rabid bird-watchers and Frisbee golfers a 115-acre green place to play. Over five miles of trails follow and diverge from Lawson's Fork Creek as it winds through this shady Shangri-la.

In early summer, the namesake Cottonwoods let loose their snowy flowers (best place to see these towering trees is near the pedestrian bridge), but there's nature galore year-round in these woods, including deer, turkeys and foxes. Check out the Loblolly, Turkeycut and Wetlands trails, where you might get lucky and see a beaver building his dam.

This preserve gets a fair amount of family traffic—and watch out when the Spartanburg Running Club thunders through!—so it's a good place to get away from it all and feel safe at the same time. There's a fabulous boardwalk trail through a wide wetlands, taking you into the heart of a birding paradise. And if chucking Frisbees is your strong suit, enter the course off Woodburn Road, 0.3 miles east of the traffic light at Fernwood Drive. (864) 948-0000, dawn to dusk daily. *spartanburgconservation.org*

BLUE WALL PASSAGE OF THE PALMETTO TRAIL

500 Hunting Country Rd, 28782

The northern part of the county features the rolling hills of the upstate, the charming town of Landrum and a gateway to the Blue Wall Preserve. The 14-mile section of trail begins in the Foothills Equestrian Nature Center (FENCE), a nature education and recreation center. Country roads and sidewalks connect the two ends of the passage, going through the heart of downtown Landrum and around lovely Lake Lanier. The last two miles are strenuous. Explore it on foot or mountain bike. *palmettoconservation.org/bluewall.asp*

PETERS CREEK PRESERVE \ *near 260 Kelly Rd, 29307*

After crossing an unglamorous power line easement, descend into quiet woods for an easy 3.6 mile hike that passes the endangered dwarf-flowered heartleaf plant (marked with orange flags), crosses and follows Peters Creek, and ends at the gorgeous ruins of Martin's Mill and dam. Clamber over the ruins at your own risk. The tall stone walls are excellent perches for deep, existential conversation. This property is downstream from the farm where Michelle Obama's great-great-great grandmother Melvinia lived as a child. *spartanburgconservation.org*

THE RAIL TRAIL

Access: 325 E. Henry St, 29302; 180 Country Club Rd, 29302

Walk, run, skate or bike this 1.9 mile paved trail and you'll be traveling the path of the very first train that came to the Hub City in 1859. The trail, which parallels South Pine and Union Streets, is located adjacent to restaurants, retail businesses and recreational facilities like the Pine Street YMCA and the Hot Spot Skate Park. A B-Cycle bike share station is located at the Henry Street end. In the works for 2015-16 is an cycle-track extension that will take the trail all the way to Barnet Park. *active-living.org*

HIKING AT CAMP CROFT

450 Croft State Park Rd, 29302

In the 1940s, hundreds of thousands of military recruits crawled over this landscape, firing howitzers and anti-tank guns and lobbing grenades as they prepared themselves for service in World War II. The soldiers—and the farmers before them—are long gone, but nature has reclaimed the area in a big way. Deer, squirrels, turkeys and all sorts of snakes and birds now live there in a forest that's been left alone for the past 70 or so years. Trails abound, some marked, some not. This is a great place to get away from it all. The topography is stunning—you will find high trails along ridges as well as lowland meanders through riverside meadows. On the Rocky Ridge Trail you'll pass through pine forests, deep hollows with heavy flora and a wide bowl through the maturing hardwoods.

One trail passes a WWII era foxhole reinforced with sandbags now covered in moss. Elsewhere—like a scene out of *Planet of the Apes*—the steel girders of an abandoned bridge rise out of an unlikely spot. You'll hike past remnants of old stone fireplaces, densely packed daffodils, rusting wash tubs and cemeteries, all reminding us of a deep human history. A new map is available with most popular trails well marked and there's a great video on the homepage. (864) 585-1283, Daylight Saving Time: Mon-Sun 7am -9pm; Standard Time: Mon-Sun 7am -6pm, extended to 8pm on Fri. *southcarolinaparks.com/croft*

MOUNTAIN BIKING AT CAMP CROFT

450 Croft State Park Rd, 29302

This is the best place in the county to play in the dirt. The Southside Trails have over 16 miles of horse-free riding. To get there, pass the main entrance to Croft State Natural Area and continue to Groce Road. Turn left, and at the parking area near the ball field you can pick up the Southside Loop Trail, which runs along the ridge before dropping into the Fairforest Creek's floodplain for about four miles. The trail then ascends back up to the ridge and returns you to the parking area, roughly 10 miles in all. All the other trails at Southside climb and descend in the interior of this loop.

The Rock Creek trail crosses over shoals on bedrock, a great place to stop and rinse in cool water. Try the High & Dry Trail for good climbs, dips, drops and a technical workout. The Lizard features a steady climb, whoops, a good drop and some high-speed jump options along with two big creek crossings.

Croft is home to the Stump Jump, a premier cross country mountain bike race.

For those with better health insurance, Idaho trail is a half-mile nut-knocker that runs across Southside Loop. There are deep ravines with nearly vertical drops that will test your shocks as much as they test your nerve. (864) 585-1283, Daylight Saving Time: Mon-Sun 7am-9pm; Standard Time: Mon-Sun 7am-6pm, extended to 8pm on Fri.

There's no shortage of riding opportunities for the Lycra crowd.

BIG-TIME ROAD BIKING

Unique to this area is The Assault on Mount Mitchell, one of the nation's most popular challenge rides for bicyclists. The big draw is the iconic, 6,578-foot summit of Mount Mitchell, the highest peak east of the Mississippi River. The Assault has gained a reputation for being one of the most challenging bike rides in the country.

Riders start way early in the morning from downtown Spartanburg. They make their way to Marion, NC, the stopping point for the Assault on Marion (for those who have any sense). The hardcore riders are just beginning the hard segment of the ride. Register early to ensure your spot. The event usually takes place in May. *theassaults.com*

If you'd rather be a spectator, you can get up close, really close, to national and international professional cyclists at Spartanburg's Downtown Criterium, which also takes place in May. This is a closed-circuit, multi-lap race that blazes through downtown. It's officially sanctioned and part of the USA CRITS Speed Week series. The half-mile course is unique with its cobblestone start/finish line and dangerously sharp right turns. It's a blast to watch and folks line the course to cheer on the racers. It's coupled with Spartanburg's largest annual festival, Spring Fling, and always becomes a street party. More cowbell! (864) 598-9638. *BikeTownSpartanburg.org*

BIKE WORX \ *1321 Union St, 29302*

A full-service bike shop located on the Rail Trail, Bike Worx carries gear and accessories in addition to a wide selection of bikes—road, mountain, street and youth. Eric and Susan Turner own the joint and give lots of time and money to support cycling in Spartanburg. All the staff are cyclists who can be found out on the roads most any day and provide expertise and advice free of charge. Check the webpage for great area rides. (864) 542-2453, Mon-Sat 10am-5:30pm. *bikeworx.net*

THE GREAT ESCAPE \ *105 Franklin Ave, 29301*

Lots of bikes, good service, professional advice and model trains—this is a one-stop shop for families with off-the-wall interests. The Escape is Spartanburg's oldest bike shop, operating since 1973, and they also have other locations in the Upstate. It's likely the only bike shop in the world that also includes a hobby shop. You'll find most anything you need for your model train, plastic model or radio-controlled vehicle along with microscopes, telescopes and a few other scientific items. (864) 574-5273, Tues-Fri 10am-6:30pm, Sat 10am-6pm. *greatescapebikes.com*

HUB CYCLE

226 S. Spring St, 29306

Need cheap wheels? This program of Partners for Active Living lends bikes for three months for a $15 deposit. The program was started to get people on recreational bikes, but many bikes are now being used for transportation. The bikes are anything from 3-speed cruisers to vintage road bikes and bomb-proof mountain bikes. Borrowers get a helmet and a lock in addition to the bike, and a professional mechanic is on duty one morning a week for tune-ups and flat repairs. (864) 598-9638, Mon & Wed 10-noon, 2-4pm. *active-living.org/borrowing-bicycles*

did you know?

RENT A SWEET RIDE

Want to take a bike ride across town but don't have a bike? B-Cycle to the rescue! Spartanburg had the first set-up in the Southeast and now there are five stations. With a credit card, rent a bike for the day ($5) or get a monthly ($15) or yearly membership ($30). These 3-speeders are truly designed to grab and go. We especially liked the built-in coffee cup holder. Bring your own helmet. For station locations: *spartanburgbcycle.com*

DUNCAN PARK BIKE TRAILS | *500 Duncan Park Dr, 29302*

Duncan Park's tree-lined circuit has long been attractive to runners and cyclists looking for a sweet, shaded, rolling road with little traffic right in town. Ball fields, including the oldest minor league stadium in the country, tennis courts and playgrounds have made it a destination for active folks for a couple of generations now.

But there hadn't been a whole lot of activity in the woods that rise from the lake, other than maybe fornicating teenagers or some other illicit use. That all changed when Eric Turner, who owns Bike Worx, a bike shop in town, and members of the Upstate Southern Off-road Bicycle Association designed and built a kind of ski area for mountain bikers. All sorts of daredevils are now finding their way to the place.

Six miles of trails wind through the woods, passing within a few feet of each other, over whoop-de-dos, jumps and pump turns on buttery smooth and carefully crafted trails. Turner says he wanted to create a "venue for kids to be able to ride bikes that's fun and safe. Turns out there's a lot of people like me that want to be kids." Pick up a map of the trails at Bike Worx (1321 Union St.), where you can also grab a handful of other maps for local road rides. Check out Eric giving an overview of Duncan Park here: *vimeo.com/moreviewmedia/duncanparktrails*

DUNCAN PARK BASEBALL STADIUM

1000 Duncan Park Dr, 29302

A lot of baseball has been played at Duncan Park since it opened in 1926. This stadium is now one of the oldest surviving wooden ballparks in America. While there's no longer a minor league team in Spartanburg, you can catch Spartanburg High School games there in the spring and an American Legion team—made up of top-notch high school players—on summer evenings. Tickets are super cheap, parking is free, and the concession stand sells Nathan's hot dogs! While you're there, soak up the history: Charles Lindbergh once appeared here, and some baseball greats got their start in this stadium, including Ryne Sandberg, Larry Bowa, Dale Murphy and Tom Glavine. *legion.org/baseball/schedule/SC*

AMERICAN LEGION MUSEUM \ *100 W. Park Dr, 29306*

Is military history your thing? While you're at Duncan Park, look for a big ol' Confederate soldier on a pedestal (who once had a prominent position downtown but moved here in 1966), and you've found the American Legion Museum, which has artifacts and exhibits from every branch of service from the First World War to the present. This is an old-fashioned museum that includes uniforms, photographs, flags, weapons and models. It's an immersive, comprehensive experience and is ably staffed by knowledgeable vets and volunteers. They also have a small area devoted to American Legion baseball. (864) 253-0376, Mon-Fri 10am-2pm.

RAIL TAIL DOG PARK \ *Union St, 29302*

Spartanburg's Rail Trail is a fantastic thoroughfare for biking, jogging or dog-walking, but sometimes a dog just needs to be a dog. The Rail Tail Dog Park is located across from the entrance to Duncan Park on Union Street. The fenced area features picnic tables, benches and even a swing, giving humans plenty of spots to rest while their canines cavort. Big dogs and small dogs alike are welcome—just be sure to pick up and dispose of any "presents" they may leave behind. Bags and trash cans are provided. Open sunrise to sunset.

TRIPLE TREE AERODROME

330 Mary Hanna Rd, Woodruff 29388

Yes, there's an aerodrome in southern Spartanburg County, and for one week in mid-May each year, Triple Tree is the Bonnaroo of radio-controlled airplanes. Billed as "the Augusta National of Aviation" this remote 400 acres between Woodruff and Enoree hosts the largest event of its kind in the world, attracting more than 10,000 aviation enthusiasts.

The number of activities at Triple Tree grows each year, from "fly-ins" of nearly 1,000 full-size private planes, to meet-ups of owners of every kind of radio-controlled aircraft you can imagine—mini-helicopters, autogyros, jets, propeller planes and more. They fill the skies doing barrel rolls, loop-de-loops and fantastic dives. Triple Tree has a lake for landing seaplanes, a giant hangar filled with rare and antique aircraft, a WWII control tower and six miles of hiking trails. Founded in 2000 by aviation enthusiast Pat Hartness, the Aerodrome features a 7,000-foot grass runway, the longest in the world. To keep it in pristine condition the runway is mowed every 48 hours (which gave rise to the Augusta National comparison). The facility is almost entirely volunteer run, with only one permanent staff member and a crew of over 100 volunteers who maintain the property and organize events.

To get into Triple Tree you have to be a member of an aviation association, or know someone who is. But trust us, the skies are full of planes down there, and there are a remarkable number of RVs rumbling down U.S. 221. If aviation is your thing, check the website for weekend events, give them a call, and talk your way in. (864) 640-6573. *tripletreeaerodrome.com*

DISC GOLF

The Spartanburg County Parks Department offers three great disc golf courses. **Shoally Creek DG Course** (591 McMillin Blvd., 29316) is regarded as the crown jewel in the Upstate. Professionally designed by industry leader Innova, this 19-hole, metal basket course features wide open and tight tree-lined layouts over rolling terrain. Professional and amateur concrete tee pads offer a good time for the serious disc golfer and the recreational dabbler. Local resident and Women's Disc Golf World Champ Sarah Stanhope has been known to frequent the course, reminding the boys that this is a game of technique as well as power. There also is a new, challenging course at **Tyger River Park** (195 Dillard Rd, Duncan, 29335) with both open and wooded holes. And south of town, visit the **Pipeline Course at the Old Canaan Road Soccer Complex**. This one is moderately hilly and heavily wooded. *spartanburgparks.org*

For a more rustic experience visit the **Cottonwood Trail Disc Golf Course** (Woodburn Rd. access at SPACE's Edwin Griffin Nature Preserve). Blending into the natural landscape, this 18-hole course with natural tee pads and wooden targets winds through the field and woods up to the banks of Lawson's Fork Creek. *spartanburgconservation.org*

There's an active group of disc golfers in the Upstate. They've got t-shirts and tournaments, and for a $10 membership fee, you can participate in such events as the Melee, the Firecracker Fling, and Upstate Glow doubles. Find your tribe at *upstatediscgolfclub.com*.

GLENDALE SHOALS | *351 Broadway St, 29346*

Glendale is easily the most scenic spot in Spartanburg County, so grab your picnic basket, your camera and your walking shoes. These 20 riverside acres have a little bit of everything: picturesque waterfalls, a pedestrian bridge, gothic-looking towers left over from a ruined cotton mill, a working vineyard, hiking trails and a spooky white mansion almost two centuries old. There's deep history in this spot.

The half-mile loop hike starts at Wofford College's Goodall Environmental Studies Center, passes rocky shoals (where you're likely to see a stately great blue heron), runs along the banks of Lawson's Fork Creek, then winds its way up a steep bluff that will make you think you're in the mountains. From here, you can follow the old path of the long-defunct Glendale Trolley in both directions. You're on the mill hill here, among the ghosts of the men, women and children who once manufactured soles of the shoes worn by Civil War soldiers.

Or for you thrill-seekers, wait till after a good three-inch Spartanburg rainfall and venture out onto the 1928 iron bridge as the raging floodwaters plunge over the dam and pound into the shoals below. The old structure literally shakes under your feet as the Lawson's Fork shows its full, muddy fury. It's a heart-thumper, we promise. Dawn to dusk daily. *wofford.edu/ goodallcenter* and *glendalesc.com*

When it's hot, head to the shoals to cool off. It's a rock-hoppin' extravaganza.

GLENDALE OUTDOOR LEADERSHIP SCHOOL

270 Wheeling Circle, 29346

This activity center in Glendale is the perfect place to climb, kayak and test your outdoor prowess. Housed in a former historic church in the old mill village, GOLS features 1,000 square feet of indoor rock climbing and space for meetings; however, the real fun begins outside, where you can choose the High Challenge TreeTop Adventure Trail with its giant swing and "islands in the sky," or the Low Challenge course, depending on how far off the ground you prefer to be. (Sorry, not available for drop-in fun—you must call ahead for reservations). GOLS, operated by the Palmetto Conservation Foundation, also offers wilderness medical courses and personal whitewater kayaking courses on the Pacolet-Lawson's Fork Blueway, an established paddle trail that follows Pacolet River and Lawson's Fork Creek. Great for corporate groups and there are some nifty adventure camps in the summer! (864) 529-0259. *setgols.org*

REBIRTH | *100 Emma Cudd Rd, 29302*

On the banks of the mighty Lawson's Fork Creek stands a twelve-foot-tall steel magnolia blossom, a sculpture installation by renowned artist and former Spartanburg resident Berry Bate. Sponsored by the friends and residents of Glendale, "Rebirth" anchors a tiny river park that has become a favorite fishing spot for locals. It also overlooks a gnarly ghost-town streetscape left over from early last century.

CITY SK8 | *339 Union St, 29306*

Worried about getting hassled for shredding? The Hot Spot Skate Park is your place. Constructed with input from local skaters, this downtown skate spot is the first public concrete park in the state. You'll find street-style features like steps, rails, ramps and ledges. The plaza section leads into a flow course that has a pyramid, and the lower section of the park is a half-pipe with escalators, a spine, camel hump and an eight-foot vertical ramp off to the side leading back into the pyramid. And it's not all 'crete—you'll find a wooden bowl along with a half pipe. It'll cost you just a few bucks to skate and you gotta wear a lid. (864) 562-4463, Mon-Thurs 3-10pm, Fri 3-11pm, Sat 11am-11pm, Sun 1-9pm. In summer they open at 9 am. *hotspotskatepark.com*

After the skate park opened in 2010, city cops got serious about stopping skating in downtown. If you get busted on your board between Daniel Morgan, Henry and Pine streets, it'll set you back $250. Yikes. And that "no skate rule" applies to both public and private property. Outside the central business district, you just have to put up with irate property owners. Forget the hassle. Head to the Skate Park where they want to see your moves.

MILLIKEN ARBORETUM \ *920 Milliken Rd, 29303*

Two hundred acres right on the edge of town have been generously opened to public access by one of the most secretive industrial companies in the world. Here you'll find people flying kites, playing ultimate frisbee, looking for love and running. Lots of running. It has become a favorite of local coaches for cross country and several major events are held here yearly. Bird watching and feeding the ducks are very popular, but watch your butt around those pesky Canadian geese. Park on the frontage road. Open daylight hours.

HATCHER GARDEN & WOODLAND PRESERVE \
820 John B White Sr Blvd, 29301

This 10-acre public botanical garden is open every day of the year and it's free. A dense oasis of plant life, Hatcher Garden grew out of the dream of a retired social service worker and his school-teacher wife who transformed a trash-filled gully into an urban refuge. A paved trail, picnic tables, ponds, a great plant collection and even a 10-foot waterfall await your visit. Whether you spend 30 minutes or three hours there, you will be inspired by the beauty and their vision. (864) 574-7724, daylight hours. *hatchergarden.org*

CLEVELAND PARK \
141 N. Cleveland Park Dr, 29303

This park has come a long way, baby. After a massive revitalization effort completed in 2004, Cleveland Park has returned to its former glory and currently boasts a pristine lake, indoor and outdoor event spaces, walking trail, geocaching trail, youth fishing club, lakeside amphitheater, bubbling creek and playground. Pack a picnic and enjoy a passive afternoon of recreation in this downtown park. (864) 562-4150, open daily during daylight hours. *spartanburgparks.org*

did you know?

GEOCACHING

Spartanburg is filled with geocaching sites. Geocaching is that high tech game of seeking "treasure" using GPS. Get started with the Heritage Geotrail where a series of caches will take you on a historical tour of the county. Explore Native American history, the Revolutionary War, King Cotton and more. Bag 16 of the 20 caches and get a limited edition, trackable geocoin. *spartanburgparks.org*

PADDLING THE PACOLET BLUEWAY

PUT IN: 190 Goldmine Rd, 29302

Now part of a 50-mile, paddle-trail "blueway" from Glendale to Lockhart, the real jewel in Spartanburg's river crown is the east side's 3.5-mile stretch of the Pacolet River from Clifton Beach to the confluence with the Lawson's Fork. There's the thrill of some mild Class II whitewater, with a chance of seeing great blue herons, wood ducks, deer, turtles, ospreys and, even once in a while, a bald eagle or an otter. Even a beginning boater can handle this stretch. There are multiple put-ins in the area of Clifton Beach—a wide, sandy spot that has hosted recreating locals for more than a century and will soon feature a massive county park. At the end of your float, Lawson's Fork Creek comes in from the right where you see a wide green cow pasture. If you see the big rocky cliff (known as Buzzard's Roost) on your right, you've gone too far. Paddle two hundred yards up Lawson's Fork and take out where you've left your second vehicle at the Goldmine bridge (2150 Goldmine Road).

If it's no-risk, lake-like paddling you're looking for, bypass Lawson's Fork and paddle another three miles, taking out on river-right at the town of Pacolet. From here, there's a terrific two-day trip to the old cotton mill town of Lockhart. You can pitch a tent overnight on sandy Goat Island, about a mile past the confluence with the Broad River. Pick up a map at Hub City Bookshop, 186 W. Main St.

TAME THE TYGER

This annual race and float on the Tyger River in southern Spartanburg County is THE whitewater paddling event in South Carolina. An April tradition, it draws paddlers from across the Southeast. After the morning downriver race and recreational float, participants and spectators are treated to local flavor in the form of BBQ and bluegrass on the banks of the Tyger River. Get your boat ready and prepare to rub elbows with river rats, first-timers, weekend warriors, local color and Spartanburg's elite. Check the website for this year's date. (864) 595-5356. *spartanburgparks.org*

VAN PATTON SHOALS \ *SC Hwy 418, Woodruff 29388*

Without a doubt, the most dramatic natural feature of the Piedmont landscape are the shoals, where rivers plunge over raw bedrock in a series of rapids and waterfalls. Situated along a sweeping bend on the Enoree River, Van Patton Shoals is one of the least visited and most breathtaking. Take a trip for kayaking, tubing or sunbathing and expect to have a blast. Access and parking are tricky, but where there's a will, there's a way! Park next to the 418 bridge at the Spartanburg/Laurens County border.

MUSGROVE MILL & HORSESHOE FALLS

398 State Park Rd, Clinton, 29325

Tucked away at the extreme southeastern corner of Spartanburg County is Musgrove Mill State Historic Site. The small Revolutionary War battle site makes the visit worthwhile for history lovers. The park's nature trail features the Enoree River, Cedar Shoals Creek and Horseshoe Falls, where legend has it that Mary Musgrove, the mill owner's daughter, hid a Patriot soldier from the British. Take Highway 56 to get there by the scenic route. (864) 938-0100, 9am-6pm daily.

did you know?

WHERE TO RENT A KAYAK

Spartanburg County has lots of water—nice lakes, lazy streams and rollicking rivers with occasional whitewater. Cody's Kayaks is the local source for kayak rentals, with a fleet that includes Dagger, Wave Sport and Perception products. They have sit-on-top, tandem and recreational kayaks and can provide all the equipment you'll need. Day rates range from $30 to $45, with a $120 deposit—and Cody's delivers. The staff also can do guided tours for up to 12 people. (864) 293-4632. *codyskayakrentals.com*

HAIR OF THE DOG \ *266 S. Pine St, 29302*

What better way to unstick that tongue from the roof of your mouth, post-NYE champagne binge than running 5 or 10 miles on New Year's morning? Chase that hangover down and stomp it dead during this scenic tour of Spartanburg neighborhoods in the wintry air. Aid stations include volunteers in tuxes handing out champagne and bling. This annual act of lunacy has been ongoing for 30+ years. (864) 585-0306, January 1. *spartanburgymca.org*

THE NU-WAY 5K \ *373 E. Kennedy St, 29302*

Can you drink beer? Can you eat Krispy Kreme doughnuts? Can you run/walk/roll/crawl 3.1 miles? If so, consider yourself ready for this battle in the urban jungle of downtown Spartanburg. The race winds through the heart of the city, with a pit stop in historic Hampton Heights where racers will find only PBR and Krispy Kreme doughnuts to fuel them: one of each must be consumed to qualify for the win. Hint: burping is key to victory. (864) 582-9685, end of October.

The NuWay 5K is not about the running. It's about the fun.

CAMP CROFT HALF MARATHON

450 Croft State Park Rd, 29302

Once an active military camp, the course treats runners to a serious beatdown on single and double track trails. While Croft's natural scenery is beautiful, keep your eyes on the trail ... or your knees and elbows will pay the price. But the reward at the end of the race is sweet: BBQ, RJ Rockers brew and a pint glass for all participants. If you want to call yourself a badass, sign up for this one. (864) 978-3378, mid-November. *campcrofthalfmarathon.com*

did you know?

THAT CREEPY GREEN VINE

The South is plagued with dense, green kudzu (CUD-zoo) vines, but Spartanburg may be the only place a cadre of hard-core kudzu fighters is actively working to KO this pesky plant. Calling themselves the Trees Coalition, they welcome new recruits: they'll dress you in the official uniform (orange vest), give you a weapon (pick ax) and take you into the kudzu patch for some serious instruction on how to beat back the vine that's been known to grow a foot a day. *treescoalition.org*

TURKEY DAY 8K

101 W. St. John St, 29302

Once you get that bird in the oven, you'll have plenty of time to stretch and prepare for this pre-feast road race. The race began as a bet between two friends and has grown to over 400 participants. Entry is free with a canned good donation. If your gobbler outfit doesn't slow you down, you might win some turkey socks. (864) 598-9638, Thanksgiving morning. *active-living.org*

SPACE JINGLE BELL RACE *500 Dupre Dr, 29302*

Ring in the holiday season with this 5k and support local land conservation efforts. The course is primarily on the Cottonwood Trail. Race day flair includes a myriad of bells, mistletoe, Santa hats and red and green running gear. This is the first in a new series call the Great SPACE Races, with the other two being longer cross-country courses on land preserved by this environmental organization. Run all three for some serious environmental cred. (864) 948-0000, mid-December. *spartanburgconservation.org*

TEXTILE TOWN TOUR

Grab a camera, hit the road and discover why Spartanburg is a textile town. A brand new, digital self-guided driving tour will give you a glimpse into the lives of the more than 100,000 men, women, and children who labored in Spartanburg County textile mills over the course of two centuries. You'll discover mills that now have a second life after significant changes in the industry, and greasy spoons that catered to the millhands. Half or full-day tour, with turn-by-turn directions at *textiletowntour.com*.

REVOLUTIONARY WAR TOUR

Did you know that South Carolina had more Revolutionary War battles than any other colony except New Jersey? Explore them with a digital, self-guided driving tour. It will take you all over the county, from Daniel Morgan's statue in the geographic center of the city, to markers in bucolic environs erected by the Daughters of the American Revolution. Half or full day tours with turn-by-turn directions at *revwartour.com*.

SPARTANBURG MUSIC TRAIL | *Downtown, 29306*

Grab your cellphone and head out on the Spartanburg Music Trail, a 30-minute outdoor walking tour of the city's incredibly robust music history. At each colorful marker you can hear the music that lifted a Spartanburg artist onto the national stage. You'll learn which Spartanburg bluesman lent his first name to British rock group Pink Floyd, who played electric guitar for Elvis Presley, who wrote "Duelin' Banjos," who was Paul Simon's sidekick on "Loves Me Like a Rock" and who put the words and music together to create the hymn "Amazing Grace." And of course you can commune with

the Marshall Tucker Band, superstars of Southern Rock, who rehearsed in the basement of an old hotel on N. Spring Street and went on to put Spartanburg on the musical map. (864) 577-9349. *spartanburgmusictrail.com*

This is one bus ride you won't soon forget!

HOLLYWILD ANIMAL PARK

2325 Hampton Rd, Wellford, 29385

Hollywild is a zoo full of celebrities. Hence the name. Here you can meet nearly the entire animal cast of the flick *Date with an Angel*, the world's only "working" rhino, cougars featured in *Last of the Mohicans*, tigers featured in *Prince of Tides* and bears featured in *A Breed Apart*. You'll know these animal celebrities from their "stars" in front of their habitats, listing their film credits. Throughout the park are petting/feeding areas with domesticated animals like alpacas, goats and sheep. But the real treat is the zany Outdoor Safari ride in an open-air bus. Climb aboard— be sure to purchase a bag of animal food —and head out into 70 acres of free-roaming deer, emu, zebra and gigantic cattle (one of which is likely to unfold his gnarly, foot-long tongue through the window).

Perhaps the most beloved creature in the park is Tank, the rare white rhino. When the safari driver tells you he weighs over 6,000 pounds and "successfully totaled 7 out of 10 Land Rovers" on a commercial shoot, you believe it. He is huge! When it gets cold outside, Hollywild has one of the best Christmas light shows anywhere. You drive your own car through the park and have a chance to hand-feed animals while seeing a spectacular light display. Check online for special offers on tickets and hours before your trip. (864) 472-2038, seasonal hours. *hollywild.org*

SPARKLE CITY MINI PUTT \ 125 E. Main St, 29306

We challenge you to find another city in America with a free, artist-designed miniature golf course in its central business district. We have news for you: the only one is right here in Spartanburg—Sparkle City Mini-Putt, the brainchild of visiting artist Robin Schwartzman and her friends at HUB-BUB, Spartanburg's alternative arts group.

Sparkle City is strictly BWOP (putter) and BWOB (ball), but there is a growing list of businesses downtown that will lend these to you, as well as give you a scorecard. All you have to do is leave your driver's license with them as you make your way around the colorful, nine-hole course in an empty lot where a movie theatre burned in the 1970s.

Schwartzman, who lives in Minneapolis, was a HUB-BUB artist in residence in 2015 who concocted the idea to create a mini-putt installation highlighting the city's drive-ins and diners. The idea grew from there to include other landmarks made by local blacksmiths—the Glendale bridge, the Hub City's railroads, Gen. Daniel Morgan, among others—and lo and behold, it became a permanent feature of Spartanburg's downtown.

Schwartzman, who runs a blog called acoupleofputts.com, says mini-golf is having a resurgence as an artist-designed movement. It brings families together and gets little Kevin's eyeballs off his iPad for a while. So grab a group and stop in at Paisley Paw, The Local Hiker, the Coffee Bar or Dottie's to get outfitted for an evening at the links, hipster style.

C&C THUNDER | *4855 S. Main St, Cowpens, 29330*

When it's time to fire up the V-Twin, head to one of the best custom motorcycle shops in the area: C&C Thunder. This shop specializes in custom-built bikes and taking your stock Harley and helping you turn it into your dream ride. They can also handle your regular maintenance and repairs (even if you ride an "import" bike, as long as it's a cruiser).

Joe, the shop's manager, showed off one of their builds to us. "The latest bike we built from the ground up is sitting right there—an 11-foot, stretched one-of-a-kind. That one is going for $25,000." You'll also find used, late model bikes for sale, whether you are looking for a bagger for that cross country haul or a Dyna for that Sons of Anarchy fix. Working on your own build? You'll find lots of parts to fix or dress up your ride. Helmets, jackets or a cool t-shirt can all be had as well.

C&C is a small shop with three guys working there. Owner Chris Jolley makes sure they are very involved in the community, sponsoring an apprentice program with Broome High School. Stop by, check out the bulletin board for info on upcoming rides, bikes for sale and chat with the fellas. You might even find a ride that catches your eye. (864) 463-7433, Tues-Fri 9am-6pm, Sat 9am-4pm.

When it's time to heed the call of the road, only a custom iron horse will do.

PLACES TO FISH

If you're an angler, there are plenty of fish waiting for you here. Lake Bowen, north of Spartanburg on I-26, is an excellent spot for largemouth bass and brim, with the caveat that it gets very crowded in the summer, and the boat traffic can make fishing more challenging. Camp Croft State Park is prime territory for bass, brim and catfish because it's constantly restocked, and they also offer boat and canoe rentals. If you're into fly-fishing, head over to Tyger-10 Park and Nature Center, 3100 Walnut Grove Road near Roebuck; in early summer, they host an awesome fly-fishing event called Fish the Tyger. And if you need some gear before hitting the river venture up to RiverBlade Knife and Fly Shop at 1398 Boiling Springs Road.

CLIMB UPSTATE | 6655 Pottery Rd, 29303

One of the largest climbing gyms in the state is right here. Over a dozen top-roping stations, 160+ feet designed for bouldering and lots of routes that will test you. They have a gymnastic floor (squishy) and crash pads, but this is top-belay at its best. No experience necessary and no reservations required, but its best if you go with a partner if you want to belay. If you love it, become a member and take advantage of their fitness area. It's your new gym! (864) 699-9967, Mon-Fri 4-9pm, Sat noon-5pm. *climbupstate.com*

HUB CITY RAILROAD MUSEUM | 298 Magnolia St, 29303

There's a reason we're called Hub City, and this is the place where you find out why. Tracing the beginnings of local railroads back to 1849 and located in Spartanburg's historic Magnolia Street Depot, this collection includes a 1940s restored red caboose, a working model train and hundreds of tools, photographs and railroad ephemera. The museum also connects the

booming railroads to textiles, peaches and Hayne Shop, a major train car repair facility once located north of town. Since it's located at the depot, it's also likely that you'll be treated to a passing freight train during your visit. Wed 10am-2pm, Sat 8am-2pm.

This iconic piece of working furniture was found in Cowpens' antique row.

SPARTAN PHOTO CENTER | *108 Garner Rd, 29303*

This is one of the few "old school" photo stores left in the area—but there is nothing out-of-date about it. This locally-owned store offers a great lineup of cameras as well as a myriad of services, including picture restoration, video-editing, in-house processing and rental equipment. Need to rent a photo studio? They have one, equipped with backdrops and lights. Bring your shoebox of old photos and these folks will put them on a CD. They also can put your favorite pictures on just about anything: t-shirts, metal, wood, water bottles, mugs and iPhone cases. (864) 583-6835, Mon-Sat 9am-6pm. *spartanphotocenter.com*

PAGES ON PINE | *2355 S. Pine St, 29302*

Just a few miles outside of downtown Spartanburg, sits a 10,500-square-foot building stocked full of used and rare books, shelved and ready for sale. Pages On Pine, a Friends of the Spartanburg County Public Libraries bookstore, sells donated books at unbelievable prices: $2 for hardcovers and $1 for paperbacks. Plus you'll find DVDs, CDs, vinyl records and VHS tapes, too. Pages is operated by volunteers, and if you love working with pre-loved books and want to lend a hand, they want to hear from you. (864) 285-9045 or (864) 585-0111. Mon-Fri noon-5pm, Sat 10am-2pm.

It's more than a bookstore.
It's a community hub.

HUB CITY BOOKSHOP | *186 W. Main St, 29306*

The *Chicago Tribune* says the Hub City Bookshop is "worth going out of your way to visit." Founded by writers, this happy place is one of a handful of not-for-profit bookstores in the whole country, meaning that every dollar spent here funds community publishing, a wide variety of creative writing educational programs and book donations to area kids.

Located in the heart of downtown, this is so much more than a bookstore. It's a virtual theme park for book lovers and aspiring authors, and a vital part of the comeback of Spartanburg's downtown. Hub City Press, an award-winning independent Southern publisher, operates here; its 70+ titles—novels, local histories, poetry books and memoirs—are featured on a wall in the front. You can sign up for writing workshops or summer camps here, and there are plenty of evening events where you can meet famous authors. And if you're looking for the best spot in town for a meeting, grab the comfy couch in the front window.

On top of all that, this is a bookstore for serious readers. Hand-picked new releases in fiction and nonfiction fill the front tables. (Don't miss the Recommended Reading wall.) There's a solid regional selection and a great children's corner. Used books are in the back. And if you're looking for Spartanburg souvenirs, this is a great place to start. (864) 577-9349, Mon-Thurs 10am-7pm, Fri-Sat 10am-9pm. *hubcity.org*

THE LOCAL HIKER \ *173 E. Main St, 29306*

Until The Local Hiker opened in late 2013, finding hiking, camping and outdoor gear meant gettin' out of town. After years of traveling the Upstate in search of supplies to satisfy their family's appetite for adventure, Michael and Kathy Silverman decided to open a shop of their own. The couple developed a business plan and won Spartanburg's highly competitive Main Street Challenge, an economic development contest designed to revitalize downtown. The accolades keep on rolling in. You may have seen the shop featured in *Backpacker Magazine*'s Get Out More Tour, an exclusive list that highlighted only 65 stores nationwide. With all your favorite brands like ENO, Patagonia and Osprey, it is easy to see why this shop is both a local and national favorite.

They have everything you need for your next great outing, whether you're thru-hiking the AT or camping in the backyard. Their motto, posted on their E. Main Street window, is "Educate, Encourage, Equip." This store is here to do more than just sell you gear. With free classes open to the public on everything from gear maintenance, to cooking in the wilderness, to Leave No Trace, The Local Hiker is committed to giving patrons not only the supplies but also the skill set to get outside and play.

Whether you've got your heart set on becoming a better steward of the earth, or the next Grizzly Man, The Local Hiker is a great resource. (864) 764-1651, Mon-Fri 10am-7pm, Sat 9am-7pm. *thelocalhiker.com*

PAISLEY PAW \ *155 E. Broad St, Suite 3, 29306*

We love our dogs and cats, and Paisley Paw is where we spoil them best. This downtown boutique has a wall of pet toys you've got to see to believe. Paisley Paw is perfect for running in to pick up a bag of dog food and locally baked dog biscuits or even treating your pooch to a spa day. The DIY dog wash comes with everything but the dog, with extra options available. (864) 327-9323, Tues-Thurs 9am-7pm, Fri-Sat 10am-5pm. *paisleypaw.com*

WILD BIRDS UNLIMITED \ *468 E. Main St, 29302*

This sunny shop provides everything that a bird lover needs to nurture and enjoy our flying feathered friends. If you need binoculars to zoom in on a far-away warbler, Wild Birds Unlimited has them, plus illustrated books to help you identify and learn about all things avian. There are bird recordings that you can sample and a varieties of gifts, including a great selection of wind chimes. Check out the children's books, hats, bird-themed greeting cards and clocks. (864) 585-0409, Mon-Fri 9:30am-5pm, Sat 10am-4pm. *spartanburg.wbu.com*

THE SCUBA SHOP \ *333 Whitney Rd, 29303*

This place owes a lot to the movies. James Cameron, writer and director, picked the Scuba Shop to work with when he was filming *The Abyss*. They've got a great selection of new gear and rentals, and they offer PADI certified classes in their indoor heated pool. When you're ready for an underwater adventure, they can take you to Florida, the islands or up to their second shop at Lake Jocassee. If you head to Jocassee, do the "graveyard dive" with them. You'll recognize it from the movie *Deliverance*. It might be hard to hear the banjo music underwater though. (864) 585-5694, Mon-Fri 10am-6pm, Sat 10am-2pm. *scubashopsc.com*

KISS THE FROG GALLERY \ *518 E. Main St, 29302*

A beautiful boutique gift shop and eclectic art gallery, Kiss the Frog carries everything from handmade jewelry and estate items to furniture, ceramic miniatures and original local art. It's owned by longtime local ad-man and confessed shopaholic Larry Souther, whose gift for gifts is a feast for the eyes. (864) 583-1309, Wed-Fri 10am-5pm, Sat 10am-3pm, during third Thursday Art Walks 6-9pm. *kissthefroggallery.com*

DOTTIE'S TOFFEE \ 155 W. Main St, 29306

Right behind the Love Where You Live mural downtown you'll find one of the many reasons we do love where we live—delicious, locally made toffee. Made with his grandmother Dot Smith's recipe, Nick Belmont has been producing toffee for the local masses since 2006, and is now reaching a global market. Up front, try a scoop of ice cream from the Wholly Cow creamery in Charleston, then head to the viewing area and watch the world famous toffee being "Handmade in Sparkle City." The toffee makes a great gift—but we won't blame you if you save it all for yourself. (864) 680-5091, Mon-Sat 10am-8:30pm. *dottiestoffee.com*

BROWN ROOF \ 141 Fernwood Drive, 29302

How many thrift stores do you know that have a "Creator of Culture and Style?" How many have fixtures from Restoration Hardware and a 30-seat coffee shop with an urban vibe? The brainchild of Robert Caldwell III, an 18-year-old high school student from a particularly artsy Spartanburg family, Brown Roof is, well, a thrift shop of a different color. Located in a former Fresh Market, this super-sized store partners with a squadron of local churches for its merchandise—clothing, furniture, etc.—then funds local charities with the proceeds. Young Mr. Caldwell has headed off to Illinois to college, but Brown Roof marches on. Mon-Fri 9am-5pm, Sat 9am-6pm. *brownroof.org*

OLIVE AND THEN SOME \ *124 Magnolia St, 29306*

If you're looking to enhance your pantry or find the perfect gift for the chef in your life, look no further than Olive and Then Some. Featuring a wide assortment of olive oils and balsamic vinegars, the friendly staff is always on hand to make recommendations for recipes or give you a sample of ice cream. Who knew you could use oils and vinegars in martinis and cakes? The entire selection is available for tasting so you can find just the right bottle for you, or you can schedule a private tasting event so you and your friends can expand your palates together. (864) 582-4442, Mon-Sat 10am-5pm. *oliveandthensome.com*

THE NEEDLE AND CANVAS \ *451-B E. St. John St, 29302*

The Needle and Canvas, located in an old fire station, boasts one of the largest selections of thread and hand-painted needle canvasses in the Southeast. With access to designers from around the country, The Needle and Canvas attracts customers from all over the Carolinas. This unique shop offers its own finished services, a variety of needlepoint accessories and quick-and-easy DIY gifts. Customers are welcome to make appointments for some special help with their current stitching projects, or to stop by and join stitching circles on Tuesdays and Thursdays. Classes and workshops are offered on demand. (864) 582-1288, Mon-Fri 10am-5pm. *theneedleandcanvas.com*

IMAGINATION STATION \ *180 E. Main St, 29306*

It's been awhile since that inner child in you was allowed to get out and play, don't you think? Do yourself a favor and head down to Imagination Station. This place was started by Marc Slotin, a guy who never wanted to grow up—and it's a great thing he didn't. He'll let you test-drive his Plasma Car (toddler up to 300 pounds) or show you how to work the Stomp Rockets, Snap Circuits and Electronic Projects. There's plenty of Hello Kitty and Gund, too. You're never too old to be a kid. (864) 573-8800, Mon-Fri 10am-5pm, Sat 10am-3pm.

JUNKIN'

Whether you're looking for furniture on the cheap or some stylish vintage duds, everybody goes junkin' every once in a while. Thrift stores provide a wealth of treasures and Spartanburg has plenty of them. Our multiple local Goodwill stores are usually somewhat organized with a majority of the store dedicated to clothing. When they do have furniture it's priced to sell and other shelf items are usually cheap, too.

The Salvation Army store on John B. White Sr. Blvd. keeps a good selection of furniture and clothing. It's a clean, large store with medium turnover but beware the boutique prices. Miracle Hill Thrift Store on Whitney Road is a little rougher around the edges but the prices are good and the donations aren't as filtered so you can find just about anything. In the same strip is Not Your Average Thrift Store, which is more of a resale/consignment store. Still, it's usually full, with lots of furniture, restaurant equipment, electronics, etc. You won't find any clothing at the Habitat Resale Store on S. Pine St., but they always have a good furniture selection as well as housewares and building supplies. The store gets quality donations but you're not going to find the best deals here. You may however find that seafoam green sink out back for your midcentury restoration.

From kitsch to quirky, second hand stores offer lots of character for your place.

"VINTAGE" CHALK ART BANK 14.95

BARNYARD FLEA MARKET \ *2000 Hwy 101, Greer, 29651*

There are many backroad resale stores, pawn shops, salvage barns, auction houses and antique stores to discover in Spartanburg County but flea markets are where it's at! Barnyard Flea Market, with 500 vendor spaces, is the newest, biggest and best. You can find just about anything here, and many vendors specialize in vintage toys, tools, bikes, restaurant equipment, music, etc. Of course you will still find the standard vendors of cheap Chinese-made plastic goods, but overall Barnyard is about as classy as a South Carolina flea market could be. (And believe it or not, it's part of a chain.) Parking can be a challenge, but this place is clean, well-maintained, and with six long, covered rows, it's pure junkin' pleasure. Thinking about selling your own stuff? You can rent a 10x10 space for $10-$19, depending on location within the flea market. (864) 968-1700, Sat 7am-4:30pm, Sun 8am-4:30pm. *barnyardfleamarkets.com*

BURR'S TRADING POST \

Corner of E. Oconee St and Old Stage Rd, Chesnee, 29323

Also known as the Chesnee Flea Market, Burr's is more of a cultural outing than a shopping trip. There are roughly 100 vendors lined up along dirt paths, some flaunting elaborate display tables with items carefully arranged while others take a more casual approach, allowing the piles of spare parts overflowing from the back of their pick-ups to speak for themselves. No

matter what you're looking for—Atari games, live animals, golf clubs, power tools—you can find it here. Plan to get there early if you don't want to end up lugging your catch a quarter of a mile back to your car; also, some vendors are gone by 10 am. Wear your boots, and don't forget to bring your manners—a sign posted at the entrance warns that drinking and profanity are not welcome. So mark your calendars and leave your booze and your cussin' at the gate. (864) 461-7967, Mon & Thurs 5am-2pm.

ANTIQUING IN COWPENS

With only one stoplight, it's not an understatement to say that Cowpens is small. Surprisingly, you'll find five antique stores within a block and half. Start off at the **Cowpens Gallery** with a free, organic, fair-trade coffee sample as you browse their selection of handmade items, antiques and custom photos. We were surprised to find handmade Guatemalan rugs and baskets in this store alongside a selection of vintage cameras. Across the street is **Lillie**'s, with 15 booths stocked by different individuals; they had quite the selection when we were there—from a full-length, camel faux-fur coat for only $95, to vintage comics, to vintage stereo cabinets with plenty of albums from the 70s to go along with them. Just a few steps away is **The Violet Box**, where we saw hand-carved decoys, some vintage silver and turquoise jewelry and an amazing pie safe that your great-grandmother would have used. Not to be outdone, **Eight Gates Antiques** is packed with treasures, even displaying merchandise in the bathroom! We really liked the gun lighter, bucket of windup alarm clocks and the classic lava lamp. They've expanded to an outdoor garden shed that holds architectural salvage, vintage garden furniture and farm items. **Vintage on Main** is the place your mom will like the best. The home decor, jewelry and candles will have her raving for weeks. All the stores are open Thursday through Saturday, and most are open during the week.

ROPER MUSIC | *551 E. Main St, Suite 106, 29302*

We stopped into the only independent music store in town expecting to find a small-town music store ... you know, small selection of overpriced items. What we found was the exact opposite.

Everywhere we looked was filled with instruments, from saxophones to electric guitars. Their floor is filled with drums, guitars and combos, and the walls sport band and orchestra equipment. There is an acoustic room featuring Taylor and Fender. There's even a ukulele section! What caught our eye was the Gretsch Brooklyn drum set on sale for $2,599. Plus there are display cases packed with reeds, mouthpieces, rosin and individuals strings.

This is a full service music store. There are eight studios in the back for individual instruction on everything from brass instruments to drum sets. They see about 250 students a week. There is a good selection of books aimed toward method and instruction for the band and orchestra crowd. Need to rent an instrument? Starting at about $20 a month you can get a clarinet for your kid or a trombone for yourself. And it's rent-to-own so all the payments go toward the purchase. If something needs fixing, these are the guys to see. They've got a great luthier to set up your acoustic and guys that can help those stuck valves on your old trumpet.

The shop is owned by Matt Roper, a good drummer in his own right and the son of local legend Jack Roper—drummer, ukulele player, magician, weatherman and TV personality. Matt worked for the biggest music stores in the area before opening his own shop in 2006. You can't go wrong shopping here. (864) 542-BAND, Mon-Fri 11am-6pm, Sat noon-5pm. *ropermusicstore.com*

BJ MUSIC DISCS & BOARDS | *374 Whitney Rd, 29303*

This music store, the best local source for vinyl, has been around since 1977 and it looks like it. You'll find a smorgasbord of hobby interest here—a couple of guitars, some drums, DJ equipment, skateboards and parts, posters and tapestries, incense and music. The music sold covers a lot of genres and comes in a lot of forms—new and used CDs, vinyl and we even spotted a couple Stanley Turrentine 8 Tracks still in the original packaging. They'll buy your old LPs and CDs and feature your band in the local music section. (864) 583-3580, Mon-Sat 10am-6pm. *bjmusicdisc.com*

THE HAY RACK | *325 W. Rutherford St, Landrum, 29356*

The Hay Rack is a kind of mini-mall for rural buckaroos or those who aspire to be the same. Step past the seed spreaders and fancy wheelbarrows on display outside into a sprawling indoor space offering everything from western and English tack to jeans and denim shirts; feed and supplements for equine, canine and feline; strange devices for distasteful tasks involving cows and pigs; hardware supplies; and a rotating crew of dogs as unofficial mascots and aisle patrollers. (864) 457-2155, Mon-Fri 8am-6pm, Sat 8am-4pm.

ARCHITECTURAL WAREHOUSE | *110 N. Trade Ave, Landrum, 29356*

Visit this spot in the northern part of the county to indulge your secret

desire to possess a "Best of Glenn Campbell" record, which would perfectly complement any of the antique mantel pieces, sideboards, desks or bookcases on display. You could furnish and accessorize a whole room, in fact, even including a door. Choose one from the many salvaged from long-gone mansions, stacked along the walls of this vast space. Be sure to pay your respects to Nelson, a Portuguese Water Dog and the official mascot. (864) 457-2199, Mon-Sat 10am-5pm, Sun 1-5pm. *architecturalwarehouse.com*

7 MOON SUPERMARKET | *1301 Asheville Hwy, 29303*

Maybe you're a fan of unconventional ramen noodle flavors like prawn and sour-hot oyster. Perhaps your tastes tend toward more accessible items like rice noodles or fresh spring rolls. No matter what your particular culinary eccentricities, you're sure to find something to broaden your culinary landscape at the 7 Moon Asian grocery store. The store also includes an Asian restaurant with some of the best Pho soup in town. (864) 804-6192, Mon-Sat 9am-8pm, Sun 9am-7pm.

ASIAN GROCERIES | *7750 Warren Abernathy Hwy, 29301*

The sign says Asian, but the merchandise is specifically Indian. Beautiful brass elephant sculptures greet you when you enter the store, and there is a display rack full of Hindu gods and goddesses, incense burners and framed art work. This is all before you get to the shelves packed with authentic Indian food, plus—this is cool—four freezers stocked with ready-to-eat meals for those who aren't into that much preparation. Tues-Sun 11am-8pm.

EUROPEAN MARKET | *8149 Warren Abernathy Hwy, 29301*

There are only two aisles, but each is replete with continental goodies. Need some Siberian dumplings? Armenian kefir? Oxford marmalade? Try the Paulaner Spezi, a can of cola mixed with lemonade, or the Lion candy bar from Poland—or fill a cart with random pickings and host an international snack party. Most items offer a handy translated label on back so you have some idea what you're buying. Their other location in Inman, at 6400 Hwy 9, stocks cakes and smoked meats as well as a selection of Cyrillic books; you're guaranteed to overhear some Russian. Mon-Sat 11am-6pm.

MI TIERRA MEXICAN FOOD MART | *7620 Asheville Hwy, 29303*

Looking to spice up your shopping list? Visit Mi Tierra for a taste of Central America. Walking up and down the aisles of this colorful little store, one can find everything from dried peppers and fresh produce to all-natural shampoos and handmade soaps. Mi Tierra also has an impressive carnicería, or butcher shop, as well as a bakery that makes enticing pastries to tempt those with a sweet tooth. (864) 503-9081, Mon-Fri 9am-8:30pm, Sat-Sun, 8am-8:30pm.

SWEET CO. | *10471 Asheville Hwy, Suite 11, Inman, 29349*

One of several Slavic grocery stores in the area, Sweet Co. stands out for its freshly baked Russian and Ukrainian cakes and pastries, along with delicious chebureki (meat pies) and salads. The shelves are filled with dried and canned goods from across Eastern Europe, along with candies and teas. Choose from a range of cold cuts and cheeses in their deli case, and enjoy the display of vintage Soviet souvenirs. If you visit more than once you're likely to see the manager, Slavic Levchenko, in a different Soviet-retro hat each time. Mon-Sat 10am-7pm, Sun 12:30-2pm.

SOUTH CHURCH STREET PRODUCE MARKET

2040 S. Church St, 29306

This produce market has everything from oranges and grapes to mustard greens and plantains. Following a personal health scare, owner Mike Fowler, a former restaurateur and chef, decided to open his own produce market. Now he describes this healthy haven as a "community health stop." All produce is certified by the S.C. Department of Agriculture's Certified Roadside Market. (864) 804-651, Mon-Sat 9am-6pm.

BELLEW'S MARKET | *240 Garner Rd, 29302*

This is a roadside produce heaven. Bellew's is where you get everything from collard greens to crookneck squash, blueberries to boiled peanuts. Walls are covered with old newspapers, and ceiling fans create a nice breeze on blistering summer days. Pick up old-time delicacies like Blenheim Ginger Ale and fruit slice candies, and don't forget a block of fatback to go with your crowder peas. (864) 585-7726, Mon-Sat 9am-6pm. *bellewsmarket.com*

SELLERS SEAFOOD MARKET | *462 W. Henry St, 29306*

In business since 1969, the market features long iced counters of fresh fish, from snapper to flounder to catfish. You can also find oysters, shucked or shelled, scallops, frog legs, crabs and even alligator meat. Take home a baggie of their breading mix, unlabeled but guaranteed to be delicious. There's also a nice selection of seafood necessities like Old Bay seasoning and homemade coleslaw, making Sellers your one-stop shop for all things fishy. (864) 583-8604, Wed 9am-6pm; Thurs-Sat 9am-7pm. *sellersseafood.com*

This is the spot for all your
gratuitous graphic gratification.

THE TANGLED WEB | *414 W. Blackstock Rd, 29301*

In a world where web comics designed to be read on iPads are moving faster than the proverbial speeding bullet through the comic publishing industry, the Tangled Web is decidedly old school. The westside comic shop started out as the Spartanburg branch of the Heroes Aren't Hard to Find chain of stores, but in 1996, when Heroes decided to shutter the location, Daniel McAbee saw his chance to turn his lifelong passion for comics into a career and bought the store.

In addition to tens of thousands of comics and graphic novels, the store also carries manga (Japanese comics), toys, figurines and Dungeons and Dragons based games like Magic: The Gathering. The store also serves as a gathering spot for Spartanburg residents sharing a passion for the comics art form, holding in-store events like costume contests and gaming tournaments.

From the beginning, McAbee wanted his store to be different from the comic shops he'd rummaged through as a customer—darkly lit and dingy, closet-sized spaces that bore little resemblance to actual businesses. "I went to shops with my then-girlfriend (now wife), and she wouldn't go inside. They were creepy, alien places to her, and she did not like that." That strategy definitely paid off, and has cemented the Tangled Web's place as Spartanburg's premier place for comics. (864) 574-1713, Mon-Sat 11am-7pm. *twebcomics.com*

PRICILLA MCCALL'S | *801 N. Pine St, 29303*

Whether you're a professional exotic dancer looking for some new ... uniforms, or just an average couple looking for some sexy lingerie, costumes, games or toys for the bedroom, Pricilla McCall's is definitely the store for you. The large, well-lit store is a cut above your run-of-the-mill adult store. Among the shop's

more quirky offerings are its wide variety of male anatomy-shaped bachelorette party favors, including Jello shot and cake molds, straws, candles and stickers. (864) 582-6997, Mon-Thurs 9:30am-9pm, Fri/Sat 9:30am-10pm, Sun noon-6pm. *priscillamccall.com*

did you know?

LIQUOR & BLUE LAWS

The drinking laws in our area are a little convoluted, so you have to pay attention if you want to drink on Sunday. Unless you're in Greer, on the far western edge of Spartanburg County, you can't buy alcohol at a store from midnight Saturday to midnight Sunday, so there's no chance to pick up a six-pack or a bottle of bourbon during those hours. But thanks to a public vote in 2014, you can head to the bars for a drink on Sunday—most in the city and county have an exemption to South Carolina's "blue laws" (it's a church thing) that allows them to serve on Sundays (except between 2am-10am).

PANDORA'S BOXXX |

*209 Westgate
Mall Dr, 29301*

Serving the carnal needs of Spartanburg's citizenry for the past nine years, Pandora's Boxxx prides itself on helping couples in the bedroom. "We resolve even the most difficult issues of intimacy for the community. We help save relationships," says store manager Jessica. If you're looking to make the best of any occasion shared with that special someone, a trip to Pandora's Boxxx is the perfect precursor to the perfect nightcap. (864) 574-6310, Mon-Sat 10am-11pm. *pandorasboxxx.net*

MOTTE & SONS BOOTLEGGING CO. | *220 E. Daniel Morgan Ave, 29302*

Bootlegging has been going on in Spartanburg for a long time. But there is no running from the law now, as the city has its first official, legal distillery with Motte & Sons Bootlegging Company. Drop in for complimentary tastings or to shop at their retail store.

Motte has a beautiful showroom with a 16-foot mahogany bar, and all their products are made on site in Spanish copper-pot stills. It's fitting that they are on Daniel Morgan Avenue, as their signature American light whiskey, distilled from corn and malted barley, is called The General. A picture of General Daniel Morgan graces the front of the bottle and a short description of his pivotal role in the Revolutionary War is on the back. The California-bred Motte family (Eugenia, Michael and four sons) also make a vodka, distilled from malted barley and malted white wheat, and a Palmetto Rum, derived from sugar cane. Their brandy is made from California white grapes. The rum is distilled from molasses and sugar cane and is barrel aged.

It's worth noting here that they call themselves bootleggers and go to great lengths on their website detailing the "Whiskey Rebellion" and Gen. Daniel Morgan's role in putting down this uprising. So there might be a wink of irony that the General's face is on every bottle of whiskey. After all, bootleggers aren't known for their respect of authority. Stop in and have a sample to see what you like. We guarantee it's the nicest bootlegging operation you'll ever come across. (864) 308-1844, Mon-Sat, 11am-7pm. *motteandsons.com*

Those pots don't make soup, but their products will make you warm and comfortable.

RUNNING SHOPS

Next time you need running shoes, don't click. Instead, choose to shop local. One of the keys to healthy running is a well-fitted pair of shoes, and now downtown has two specialty running shops to help you out. And "well-fitting" doesn't mean just the right size. A good running shop will give you professional advice about the best shoes to wear for your gait, training goals and intensity. All of us have funny hitches in our giddy-ups, and no matter your running level, the best shoes will give you the support you need to keep running injury-free. You can't get that kind of analysis online.

Both these shops opened their second stores in Spartanburg, having previously established themselves in Clemson and Greenville. **Gotta Run Spartanburg**, 159 S. Pine St., and **Spartan Running Company**, 351 E. Henry St., have brought their expertise to a town with lots of runners and active folks.

Staffed by runners, these shops give you a place to talk about training along with lots of choices on great gear and shoes. Enthusiastic, knowledgeable and personable, these folks find nothing more interesting in their day than getting you into the shoes and gear you need for getting off the couch, or stepping up your game. They know where to run in Spartanburg and can tell you about upcoming races.

Gotta Run Spartanburg (864) 345-2237, Mon-Wed & Fri 10am-6pm; Thu 10am-7pm; Sat 10 am–4pm. *gottarunspartanburg.com*

Spartan Running Company (864) 541-7444, Mon-Sat 10am-6pm. *spartanrunningcompany.com*

SMOKE 'EM IF YA GOT 'EM

If you want a good cigar, you have two choices ... go east or go west. On the east side of town in a converted house you'll find the **Tobacco Nook** (3006 E. Main St, (864) 579-2223). When you walk in you realize this is THE place if you are a roll-your-own cigarette person. The whole front is filled with loose tobacco and rolling materials. But you'll also find over 80 different labels of cigars in their walk-in humidor. On the west side is **Sir Tom's Tobacco Emporium** (2811 Reidville Rd, (864) 587-1566). No cigarettes to be had here, only premium cigars, pipes, tobacco and accessories. They are known for their in-house, professionally blended pipe tobacco and tremendous selection of cigar lines. From Fuentes to Opus X, they've got the classics plus more.

If vaping is your thing, there are more options: **Vapor Emporium & Gift Shop** (505 E. Main St, (864) 541-7860) is family run and it feels like it. Mom does monogramming and both daughters do handicrafts, plus you'll find work by local artists for sale. Oh yeah, they carry Green Smoke e-cigs. If you like the rock music pumping and your staff pierced and tattooed, head to **Carolina Vapor** Mill (807 N. Pine St, (864) 585-8526) and belly up to the "tasting bar"

where you can try out flavors from their in-house mixing station. If you are looking to hotrod your atomizer, then **The Hub City Shop** (435 E. Main St, Suite E, (864) 327-9415) is your place. They build Chump boxes, modify them and do rebuilds. You'll find hemp bracelets, tapestries, tie dyes and hookahs here as well that will remind you of smoke shops of the old days.

Pineview Drive is a sight to behold.

PINEVIEW DRIVE YARD ART | *2004 Pineview Dr, 29307*

Not everyone fills his yard with mannequins, a miniature mill village and the Statue of Liberty. When asked about the eclectic collection of artistic creations in his yard, C. C. Wheeler gets right to the point. "It's my history," he says. Now over 80 years old, he still spends his days recreating—in his suburban yard—the images from his past in interesting and unusual ways.

DUELING KRISPY KREMES |

Yes, we have two Krispy Kreme doughnut shops right across the street from each other—one a bustling, modern, round-the-clock coffee/doughnut manufacturing emporium and the other a shuttered, green-tile monument to "hot now" kitsch. Grab a glazed beauty at 351 N. Church Street, then walk over and peek in the window of the original shop, built in 1969. (864) 585-1956. *krispykreme.com*

THE BERLIN WALL | *951 Simuel Rd, 29301*

You don't have to go to a museum to see the Berlin Wall—just drive right up the Interstate in Spartanburg. When the infamous wall finally came down in 1989, Menzel, a German-owned machinery maker, purchased two graffitied sections, shipped them to its corporate headquarters in Spartanburg, and erected them facing Business I-85, complete with plaques quoting JFK and Ronald Reagan. (864) 576-5690.

Join the parade and join the party.
You'll undoubtedly run into folks you know.

UPSTATE PRIDE MARCH AND FESTIVAL

Peter Greenberg, one of the most respected travel writers in America, says the annual LGBT pride march in Spartanburg is one of the five "most unusual" festivals of its kind in the world— along with those in Istanbul, Sri Lanka, Tijuana, and Sligo, Ireland. Greenberg, like many others, is amazed that a small city in the South can host a gay pride march of this magnitude.

Since 2009, Spartanburg has been home to the Upstate Pride March and Festival held every year on a Saturday in September. The march typically draws more than 3,000 participants. There used to be a fair number of protesters, but they have all but faded away as the colorful crowds have grown. Instead, hundreds of straight people join their LGBT friends, carrying balloons, honking horns and hoisting clever signs as they wind their way through downtown Spartanburg.

One of the regular speakers at each parade is Spartanburg's Mayor Junie White. A 70-something, Southern-born, service station owner isn't the first person you'd expect to be an ardent defender of LGBT rights, but the city's mayor has made a habit out of doing the unexpected. In 2010, Mayor White made national news when he issued a proclamation recognizing LGBT Pride Day in the city. "Everybody is entitled to certain rights in these United States," he says. *upstatepridesc.org*

WOMPUS WOODS | 330 Parris Rd, Cowpens 29330

This haunted trail is legendary among local thrill-seekers, and it draws huge crowds all through October. The wooded walk includes structures, elaborate sets and an impressive cast of characters. This 30-minute Halloween experience is worth the long line, and if you're lucky, you'll get to see the Wompus beast himself. Refreshments, souvenirs, hayrides and VIP tickets are also available, and groups are especially encouraged. (864) 578-6175, October hours: Sun and Thurs dusk-11pm; Fri and Sat dusk-2 am. *wompuswoods.com*

THE SPARTANBURG GHOST TOUR |

Die-hard Halloween fans can do no better than to take one of the Main Street Trolley's annual ghost tours. Offered in October, these quirky bus tours may be loose on history, but they're definitely a good time. Stories range from grisly to laughable, and overhead monitors show photos and video of paranormal activity. Cameras are encouraged. Standard tours leave from the Magnolia Street Railroad Depot (298 Magnolia St, 29303), but special tours can be arranged for large groups. (864) 574-9876. *mainstreettrolley.com*

OAKWOOD CEMETERY | *Oakwood Ave, 29302*

If you enjoy pleasant walks in a morbid AND beautiful setting, Oakwood Cemetery is your best bet. Begun in the 1880s, it quickly became the cemetery of choice for Spartanburg's ex-movers and shakers. Browse the headstones for a who's who of old Spartanburg. Ghost sightings are reported occasionally, but you're unlikely to find much more than fresh air and funerary art.

WALNUT GROVE PLANTATION | *1200 Otts Shoals Rd, Roebuck 29376*

Whether or not you believe the stories about ghostly figures roaming the grounds, or the mysterious lights in the cemetery through the woods, Walnut Grove is worth a visit around Halloween or any other time of year. One of the oldest homes in Spartanburg County, and the site of a Revolutionary War skirmish, Walnut Grove is a meticulously restored Upcountry plantation, open for tours to the public. Visit in early October to see colonial demonstrations and battle reenactments. (864) 576-6546. *spartanburghistory.org*

ACUPUNCTURE

Ancient Chinese medicine is practiced right here in Spartanburg. If you're looking for some pain relief in the Eastern holistic way—with needles to your skin—you have several acupuncture practices to choose from. Shawn Jacobs, at the **Acupuncture Center of Spartanburg** (753 E. Main St, (864) 948-9950) is the most established. She's also a soap maker and we can't say enough about the aroma at this place! You also can get treatment with Betty Shuford, who came here from New Mexico, at **Pine Street Acupuncture** (364 S. Pine St, (864) 541-9645) or in Duncan with Simon Cairns at **Acupuncture Solutions** (220 Freeman Farm Road, (864) 613-4927).

did you know?

ADJUSTMENTS R US

The Spartanburg area may have more chiropractors per capita than any place in the world. In fact a quick Google search lists 223, more than one for every dozen residents. What's fueling this spinal adjustment craze? Since 1973 Spartanburg has been home to Sherman College of Chiropractic at 2020 Springfield Road, 29316. With nearly 400 students representing 46 states and 17 foreign countries, the college also has a Health Center providing 30,000 patient visits a year at $15 a visit, or $10 with student ID. (864) 578-8777. *sherman.edu*

YOGALICIOUS

161 Dunbar St, 29306

YOGAlicious recently moved to an intimate studio on Dunbar Street in order to better fulfill its mission of offering quality yoga instruction at affordable rates. Spartanburg's oldest studio is grounded in strong karma and kula traditions, and co-owner Adrienne Ables routinely teaches free community classes in the downtown square. Here, gentle beginner classes and rigorous vinyasa flow classes are both offered as well as workshops and series. Be prepared to slip your shoes off at the door as the front door leads directly into the yoga space. Classes offered daily. *yoga-licious.com*

SOUL FLOW YOGA | *2811 Reidville Rd, Ste. 12, 29301*

"Feel your breath, respect your body, honor your soul," is the mantra at Soul Flow Yoga, a calming gray oasis located off busy Reidville Road. There, yogis will find a welcoming community and variety of classes suitable for novices and regular practitioners alike. Daily classes are punctuated seasonally with fun, innovative workshops pairing yoga and libations such as "Wine and Unwind" and "Mountain Poses and Mimosas." Classes offered daily. (864) 609-7689. *soulflowyogi.com*

ZEN GARDEN YOGA | *1040 Fernwood-Glendale Rd, Ste 58, 29307*

Zen Studios, located at the back of Hillcrest Shopping Center, offers twenty-plus yoga and barre classes weekly, including several popular antigravity yoga classes, as well as workshops and teacher training. In addition, it is a full-service spa offering therapeutic massage, acupuncture and Reiki, and their eco-chic boutique features yoga togs, jewelry and spa essentials. Be sure to imbibe in a complimentary après yoga coffee or tea. Classes offered daily. (864) 583-3335, classes 7 days a week. *zengardenyoga.com*

PINK ANDERSON'S GRAVE \ *2310 Cannons Campground Rd, 29307*

Pink Anderson was a Spartanburg-based piedmont blues singer who influenced everyone from Johnny Cash to Pink Floyd (who used part of Anderson's name to form their own). His final resting place is in an unassuming grave in Lincoln Memorial Gardens on Cannons Campground Road. Coming from town, the cemetery will be on the left, and his grave is under a broad-leafed oak tree near the graveyard's first entrance. Bring along a guitar, and some "greasy greens" for a little picnic to salute Spartanburg's greatest bluesman.

THE DRAYTON GRAVES \ *30 Ansel St, 29307*

Be careful making the curve on Ansel Street in the Drayton mill village, you might hit someone. Well, not exactly someone. William Poole, one of the earliest residents of the area, is buried under the mound in the middle of the road along with someone presumed to be his wife. The fragments of his gravestone—death date 1808—are still on the site. Apparently a road was put through this graveyard around 1930, and the builders couldn't find heirs who could approve moving the two graves. The solution? Pave the road around them.

MARSHALL TUCKER BAND GRAVES \
1300 Fernwood-Glendale Rd, 29307

Known in the 1970s for such songs as "Can't You See," "Fire on the Mountain" and "Heard it in a Love Song," Spartanburg's Marshall Tucker Band was one of the era's biggest Southern Rock bands. Sadly, three of the band's original members passed away, and are buried in Spartanburg's

Greenlawn Cemetery on Fernwood-Glendale Road. The graves of Toy Caldwell, Tommy Caldwell and George McCorkle are scattered throughout the large cemetery, so the best bet is to ask the staff at the cemetery's office for help. They're more than happy to accommodate, and will even print out a map to help you find your Southern Rock heroes. (864) 582-1249, Open daily 8:30am-5pm.

*This is the place
where tan lines go to die.*

CAROLINA FOOTHILLS NUDIST RESORT

90 Carolina Foothills Dr, Chesnee, 29323

Carolina Foothills is a campground and resort with the kinds of amenities one might expect to find: RV spots, cabins for rent, a saltwater pool, a hot tub, a volleyball court, picnic areas and an indoor clubhouse with a pool table. The difference at Carolina Foothills isn't the resort—it's the people. Everyone at Carolina Foothills is nude.

That means no doors on the campground showers (Why would you need them?). It means skinny dipping in the pool or hot tub isn't just allowed, it's required. It means applying sunscreen in places most people never have to bother, and taking more care when using the barbecue grill than usual.

Nude recreation is the name of the game at Carolina Foothills, and whether you spend your time hanging out by the pool, or challenging your neighbor to a game of cornhole, you can be sure that no matter what you're doing, you'll be doing it au naturel. Carolina Foothills is a family friendly resort, and performs background checks on all guests to ensure safety, meaning no funny-business is allowed or tolerated. But for those looking to kick back in the sun without having to worry about buying the latest in outdoor summer wear, Carolina Foothills offers guests a chance to let it all hang out. (864) 461-2731, Office hours: Mon-Sun 9am-5pm. *carolinafoothills.com*

EASTERN RELIGION

There are things you'd expect to find deep in the woods of the Upstate: creeks, trees, maybe a bait and tackle store—but a Buddhist temple? How about three? **Wat Sao Sokh San** (841 Shiloh Church Rd, 29385) is a three-story gold and red Cambodian Buddhist stupa in Wellford, just west of Spartanburg. The building, though highly unlikely and out-of-place, is intricately detailed and quite beautiful. The stupa is meant as a pilgrimage site for all Buddhists, but the general public is welcome as well. Near Boiling Springs but still off the beaten path, **Wat Preah Ang Thom**, otherwise known as the **Spartanburg Buddhist Center of South Carolina** (770 Bryant Rd, 29303), has a variety of buildings on a nine-acre lot, including an impressively large statue of the Buddha himself. They offer a daily schedule of chanting, meditation and prayer, and there's an English-language meditation, brief Dhamma talk and group discussion on Thursday evenings. Additionally, the **Wat Lao Buddha Mettram** is at 478 Fox Road, 29306. Meanwhile, the **Hindu Society of Spartanburg** (1130 Fairview Church Road, 29303) also has a spacious temple that offers extensive holiday celebrations and daily worship, as well as a newsletter on upcoming events.

CAROLINA SPIRITUAL SCIENCE CENTER | *165 B Metro Dr, 29303*

Tucked away in a Spartanburg office park, the Carolina Spiritual Science Center has been catering to "sincere spiritual seekers" for nearly 30 years. There are semester-long classes on post-earthly life, world religions, spiritual healing and more. This is where you find your own path to intuitive knowledge of the oneness at the source of all. (828) 817-1193. *carolinaspirit.org*

did you know?

FIREWORKS

Maybe it is because of our Revolutionary War heritage, but we love fireworks here. All holidays are celebrated with fireworks. If you aren't shooting them, your neighbors will be (outside the city limits). And SC has more liberal laws than GA & NC, so you'll find massive stores near our borders. You have to be 14 to buy, unless you have a parent with you. So grab the biggest box of mortars you can find and light up the night sky.

THE DEADLY DOLLS

Roller derby has come to Spartanburg. That's right—full contact roller skating. About 20 ladies suit up twice a week for practice. It starts with yoga and stretching then moves on to jumping, walking, falling—all on skates. These girls train. They have to pass official skills test to compete. If you wanna kick some butt or just watch it happen, you should check them out. Catch them at the Skate Palace, 2345 S. Pine Street, 29302. Auditions are held periodically and bouts with other teams happen much more often. *deadlydollsderby.com*

NORTH WOODS FARMS | *519 Weatherly Rd, Inman 29349*

Simply getting to North Wood Farms might be half the fun. You cruise through charming small-town Inman, past old mills and peach farms, into a neighborhood of narrow roads and new houses, until you crest a hill and ta-da! Alpacas! A whole herd of them, regarding you with their long-lashed, eerily adorable eyes. Visitors are encouraged to pull over and take pictures, but don't  expect any great selfies—the animals are friendly but shy. When you've gawped enough, be sure to check out the yarn shop, which boasts innumerable skeins in every imaginable weight and color. Items around the store have tags with instructions on how to recreate your own shawl, hat, scarf or vest. For a warehouse in the boonies, the store is remarkably cozy, and there's often a group of women chatting on the various couches and armchairs as they crochet and knit. The store also houses its own fiber mill for processing the alpacas' wool, which they shear every May. Classes on knitting, dip-dyeing, wool-felting and more can be found at their website, where they also offer alpaca yarn for sale. (864) 906-7134, Tues-Sat 10am-5pm; Thurs Sit & Knit 6-8pm. *northwoodsfarm.com*

THE PACOLET HORSE | *100 Limestone St, Pacolet 29372*

A life-size fiberglass stallion rising out of the river welcomes you to the town of Pacolet, and you can visit him from the Highway 150 bridge in the old cotton mill town. He's a tribute to all things Pacolet—the long-shuttered mills, the textile baseball team and the old high school all used Trojan horses as their symbols and mascots. The wire cage? Protection against wiseguys chucking items at its underbelly. There are plenty of historic sites to see in Pacolet, so while you're down there, stop in at the nearby town hall and museum. Town Hall: (864) 474-9504, Mon-Fri, 9am-5pm. *townofpacolet.com*

THE UNDERGROUND GUIDE IS BROUGHT TO YOU BY

 Celebrating its 20th anniversary in Spartanburg, the Hub City Writers Project serves readers and writers through its independent press, community bookshop, and diverse literary programming. Modeled after the Depression-era Federal Writers Project, Hub City seeks to foster a sense of community through the literary arts. Since its founding in 1995, Hub City has published more than 70 books and 700 authors and is particularly interested in books with a strong sense of place.

Always doing. We are doing more because we were raised to do nothing less. That's why Spartanburg is always doing.
cityofspartanburg.org

Stuff like this only happens in a place that is truly revolutionary. Come see for yourself.
visitspartanburg.com

ABOUT THE EDITOR

Joe C. Mullinax grew up in Spartanburg and after graduating from the University of South Carolina with a degree in English and advertising, he couldn't wait to leave the state. He lived and worked in Yellowstone National Park, San Francisco and Los Angeles as a chef, music retail manager and promotion-guy for Guitar Center. He returned to South Carolina many years later and now, with a different perspective, finds it quite delightful. He is the principal at MoreView Media. When he's not doing that, he's busy being a husband, a dad and making an awful racket with drums or a ukulele.